Primary Science
in a Nutshell

Leigh Hoath & Ben Rogers

Copyright © Millgate Publishing 2024

First published 2024 by Millgate Publishing.

Millgate Publishing is the publishing arm of
The Association for Science Education
College Lane
Hatfield
AL10 9AA

The right of Leigh Hoath and Ben Rogers to be identified as the authors of this work has been asserted in accordance with the Copyright, Designs and Patent Act 1988.

Typesetting and Graphic Design by Karen Dyer

Cover design by Laura Townsend

Stock images courtesy of Shutterstock and Pixabay

Printed and bound in Great Britain by Ashford Colour Press

ISBN 978-1-915615-30-5

British Library Cataloguing in Publication Data

A catalogue record for this book is available from the British Library.

Contents

Welcome to *Primary Science in a Nutshell!*   1

The characteristics of living things   4

Classifying living things   6

Vertebrates and invertebrates   8

Mammals   10

Insects   12

Microorganisms   14

Life cycles   16

Food chains and webs   18

Leaves and photosynthesis   20

Flowers   22

Pollination   24

Fertilisation   26

Seed dispersal   28

Stems   30

Roots   32

What is soil?   34

Habitats and ecosystems   36

Natural selection   38

The senses   40

Muscles   42

Respiration   44

Digestion   46

Blood circulation   48

Solids, liquids and gases   50

Changes of state   52

Separating mixtures   54

The properties of materials   56

Metals   58

Reversible & irreversible changes   60

Forces   62

Motion   64

Forces acting at a distance   66

Light	68
Sound	70
Waves and vibrations	72
The solar system model	74
Circuits	76
Electrical conductors & insulators	78
Charge and current	80
The 'rope' circuit model	82
Energy	84
How we can protect the environment	88
Global warming	90
Climate change	92
Carbon dioxide & oxygen	94
The carbon cycle	96
The water cycle	98
Rocks	100
Classification of rocks	102
The rock cycle	104
Erosion	106
Earthquakes	108
Fossils	110
Geological deep time	112
Volcanoes	114
How to weigh things	116
How to use a thermometer	118
Measuring time	120
How to use a microscope	123
How to measure the volume of liquids	126
How to use forcemeters	128
How to manage lessons with circuits	130
Representing data	132
How to manage a science cupboard	135
Glossary	136

About the authors

Leigh Hoath

Leigh is a Professor of Science Education, bringing a wealth of experience from her time as a classroom teacher to her current role in academia. With numerous publications in both primary and secondary science education, Leigh has an established profile in this area.

Her work focuses on empowering science teachers who may lack confidence in science, emphasising the crucial role of subject knowledge in effective science teaching and learning. Leigh's approach to science education is rooted in the belief that a solid foundation of knowledge is key to building teacher confidence and, in turn, enabling young minds to explore the wonders of science. She hopes that is what this collaboration with Ben achieves.

Leigh is also Co-Founder of Climate Adapted Pathways for Education (CAPE) and seeks to equip teachers and school leaders with the knowledge to help all children and young people to take climate action and protect the environment. She has played key roles within the Association for Science Education as Editor of *Primary Science*, Chair of the Publications Committee and national Co-Chair of the Association.

Ben Rogers

Ben is Director of Curriculum and Pedagogy for Paradigm Trust and an experienced science teacher at both primary and secondary. He taught secondary school science (physics) for 18 years before becoming a primary teacher. He is an advocate for a knowledge-rich primary science curriculum and keen supporter of science subject knowledge enhancement for primary colleagues.

Ben has served on Ofsted's Science Evidence Review Panel and the EEF Primary Science Steering Group.

Ben is the author of *The Big Ideas in Physics and How to Teach Them* and writes posts on science education at readingforlearning.org

Thanks

This book was written by many hands. We would like to thank the following colleagues who contributed chapters and who helped to proofread the final document.

Sarah Bryant
David Church
Laura Dickinson Rogers
Leigh Hoath
Emily Montenero
Lewis Morgan
Caroline Neuberg
Ben Rogers
Katja Rudden
Alex Sinclair
Charles Tracy
Bryony Turford
Paul Tyler

Warning – this is NOT a curriculum!

This book was not written as a primary science curriculum. There is content that goes beyond the primary curriculum and is included to support teacher knowledge.

Testimonials

Every so often I come across a book or resource that is so elegant, so fruitful and so concise, that I start fizzing with all the ways that I might incorporate it into my practice. 'Primary Science in a Nutshell' is one such resource. Written by two experts who are absolutely at the top of their game, Ben Rogers and Leigh Hoath have delivered a brilliant summary of all the great stuff we can learn in primary science, masses of questions which will open up the terrain for pupils, plus one of the most underestimated avenues into learning: unpacking misconceptions. Absolute gold!'

Mary Myatt, Education writer and speaker

Primary science in a nutshell does exactly what it says on the tin. It gives primary teachers, some of whom may have a rather hazy understanding of scientific concepts, an overview of all of the topics in the science National Curriculum in a way that is clear and concise. Each section starts by explaining what the big idea is. Common misconceptions are highlighted and addressed and the progression between key stages is signposted. This is a book that every primary teacher trainee should have and that experienced primary teachers would also benefit from.

Clare Sealy, Head of Education Improvement, States of Guernsey.
Ex head of St Matthias primary, Tower Hamlets

Welcome to Primary Science in a Nutshell!

This book has been driven by reports over the years that suggest that primary teachers often lack confidence in teaching science. The purpose of this book is to help address this issue – but by no means solve it.

Science is challenging for learning because it involves pupils reconstructing their understanding of concepts – such as mass – and is often abstract in nature, so we need to create images in pupils' minds in order for them to grasp concepts. The other challenge that often comes up in relation to teacher confidence is that of subject knowledge, and this is where we hope *Primary Science in a Nutshell* will help.

The book chapters follow a format that takes you through the big ideas associated with the key concepts taught within the English National Curriculum and draws upon established work from people such as Wynne Harlen and Jasper Green. The chapter then outlines some of the key knowledge that the pupils need to know in order to make sense of the concept being presented – some of this will extend beyond the National Curriculum statement itself in order to ensure that you have all you need to be able to teach it. We thought that it was important to include common misconceptions that pupils often bring to lessons and ways in which these can be addressed. It is worth a mention at this point that to move pupils' misconceptions to being 'corrected' takes many visits to the same knowledge – the EEF has produced some good reading to support this, which is worth taking the time to look at.

Within the chapter, we have also included some questions to ask and, something that we feel is very important, a progression grid. This shows how the content of each topic tracks through from the Early Years to Key Stage 3 (ages 11-14) – and the reason for this is that, although you may be teaching about plants in Year 3 (ages 7-8), it is important that you are able to help pupils to make links with what they have in terms of prior learning to build on the conceptual knowledge that they already hold. And we also know that, unless you make this explicit for them, they will deny all knowledge of being taught something in the past!

The chapters are short – they are not meant to give you everything that you need to know about science knowledge. They are designed to be a 'pick-up and prep' at the planning stage and, in the short term, before teaching a lesson. It is a buoyancy aid for those who feel that they are drowning in the volume of 'knowing' that they need in order to best teach primary science.

The book is designed to be **used**. Scribble in the margins, add to the page, identify which of the pages you haven't looked at and question why! We hope that *Primary Science in a Nutshell* will enable primary teachers to feel that bit more confident as they walk in to teach that lesson that they've previously dreaded doing.

It has been written by a wealth of primary science experts from the sector – many of whom are teachers themselves. This is a distilled version of everything that you need to know...

Why primary teachers need secure subject knowledge

Subject content knowledge is crucial for primary school teachers for many reasons:

- Explaining concepts: Teachers with strong content knowledge can accurately explain scientific concepts, which helps pupils to understand and retain these ideas. Knowledgeable teachers can break complex ideas into smaller units and find multiple ways to explain when necessary.

- Answering questions: Children ask questions about scientific phenomena. A teacher with a strong knowledge base can provide accurate, understandable answers, fostering pupils' curiosity and promoting scientific thinking.

- Preparing lessons: Teachers need to understand the material thoroughly to design effective lessons and learning activities. Understanding the content allows teachers to anticipate common misconceptions and plan strategies to address them.

- Describing practical applications and examples: Teachers who understand the content can show pupils how scientific principles apply to everyday life, making learning more relevant and engaging.

- Confidence and enthusiasm: Teachers who are confident in their subject knowledge can communicate their enthusiasm for the subject to their pupils. This can help to motivate pupils and make the learning experience more enjoyable.

- Building on prior knowledge: Science is cumulative, meaning that understanding new concepts often relies on understanding previous ones. Teachers need a deep understanding of scientific concepts to guide pupils in building their knowledge progressively.

- Assessment of pupil understanding: Teachers need a strong understanding of the subject matter to accurately assess pupils' knowledge and address any gaps or misconceptions.

- Continual learning: teachers with secure knowledge foundations are able to learn and understand new ideas more readily.

- Modelling scientific enquiry: Science isn't just a collection of facts – it's a way of thinking and understanding the world. Teachers with a strong understanding of science can model the process of scientific enquiry, teaching pupils to think critically, ask questions and seek evidence.

We hope that this book will support primary teachers to teach science with confidence, enthusiasm and curiosity.

The characteristics of living things

The big idea about the characteristics of living things is that all life, no matter how big, small, simple, or complex, has specific features in common. These include the ability to grow, reproduce, react to changes in their environment, adapt over time, and maintain a stable internal environment (a concept that biologists call homeostasis).

To make the most of these ideas, start by thinking about these characteristics in organisms with which your pupils are familiar, such as humans, pets, or plants. Engaging in practical activities, such as observing how a plant grows, can make these abstract ideas more real. Encourage your pupils to spot these traits in different organisms, which will help them to see how these characteristics connect all forms of life. Using real-life examples and practical activities, such as seeing how a plant turns towards light, or how a chick grows over time, can make it easier to understand and remember these concepts.

The main challenge in learning about the characteristics of living things is that these concepts can be quite abstract and complex. They're not always easy to see or touch, which can make them problematic to grasp. It is difficult to observe these characteristics in some living things (for example, lichen or fungi) and many non-living things also share some of the characteristics of living things, so pupils may struggle to correctly classify them. To overcome this, focus on the most common examples and remember that there are always exceptions. The goal isn't to cover every example, but to build a solid foundation of understanding about what it means to be 'alive'.

Key questions

O **Can you name some characteristics that all living things share?**

O **Can you give an example of a living thing and explain how it shows these characteristics?**

O **How do living things respond to their environment? Can you give an example?**

O **What does it mean when we say that living things 'grow'? Can you give an example?**

O **Why is it important for living things to reproduce?**

O **How do living things adapt to changes in their environment?**

Common misconceptions

O **Movement equals life.**
Many pupils believe that anything that moves is alive. This is often due to the observable movement in animals. However, this leads to misunderstandings, such as thinking that cars or clouds are alive because they move.

O **All living things can be seen with the naked eye.**
Some pupils struggle with the concept that living things can be too small to see without a microscope, such as bacteria or viruses.

O **Plants are not alive.**
Because plants don't move around like animals, and their growth and responses are usually slow, some pupils don't perceive plants as living organisms.

O **Only animals eat.**
Children sometimes think that because plants don't have mouths, they don't eat. The concept of photosynthesis, where plants make their food using sunlight, is often a new idea.

Progression

Key Stage	Development of ideas
EYFS	· Pupils should experience the natural world around them, including plants and animals. They should begin to notice similarities and differences in relation to living things and start to categorise them.
KS1 (ages 5-7)	· Pupils learn to identify and name a variety of common plants and animals in their local and wider environment. They should understand that most living things live in habitats to which they are suited and describe how different habitats provide for the basic needs of different kinds of animals and plants.
LKS2 (ages 7-9)	· Pupils should begin to classify living things into broad groups based on observable characteristics and based on similarities and differences. They should also learn how environments can change and how this can affect living things.
UKS2 (ages 9-11)	· Pupils should learn about life cycles of various animals and plants and understand the process of reproduction in animals and plants. They should learn about adaptation over time and how it enables living things to survive in their environment.
KS3 (ages 11-14)	· Pupils should deepen their understanding of a wide range of scientific ideas, including cell biology (the fundamental unit of life), body systems, reproduction, genetics, and evolution. They should understand how these factors interrelate in complex ways to form the characteristics of living things.

Classifying living things

The big idea about the classification of living things is that all organisms on Earth are grouped based on their similarities and differences. These groups form a hierarchy, from broad groups such as animals and plants, down to very specific species. This classification helps scientists communicate about and understand the different forms of life on our planet.

To make the most of this idea, you should first focus on familiar organisms. Ask pupils to group different kinds of animals or plants based on specific characteristics, such as the number of legs and body sections, whether they have a backbone (photos of animal skeletons are helpful for this) and whether plants have flowers or not.

The key problem in teaching the classification of living things is the complexity and depth of the subject. Pupils may find it challenging to grasp the various levels of classification and the scientific terminology associated with it. To overcome this challenge, it's crucial to break down the topic into manageable pieces, starting from basic grouping activities and gradually introducing scientific classification.

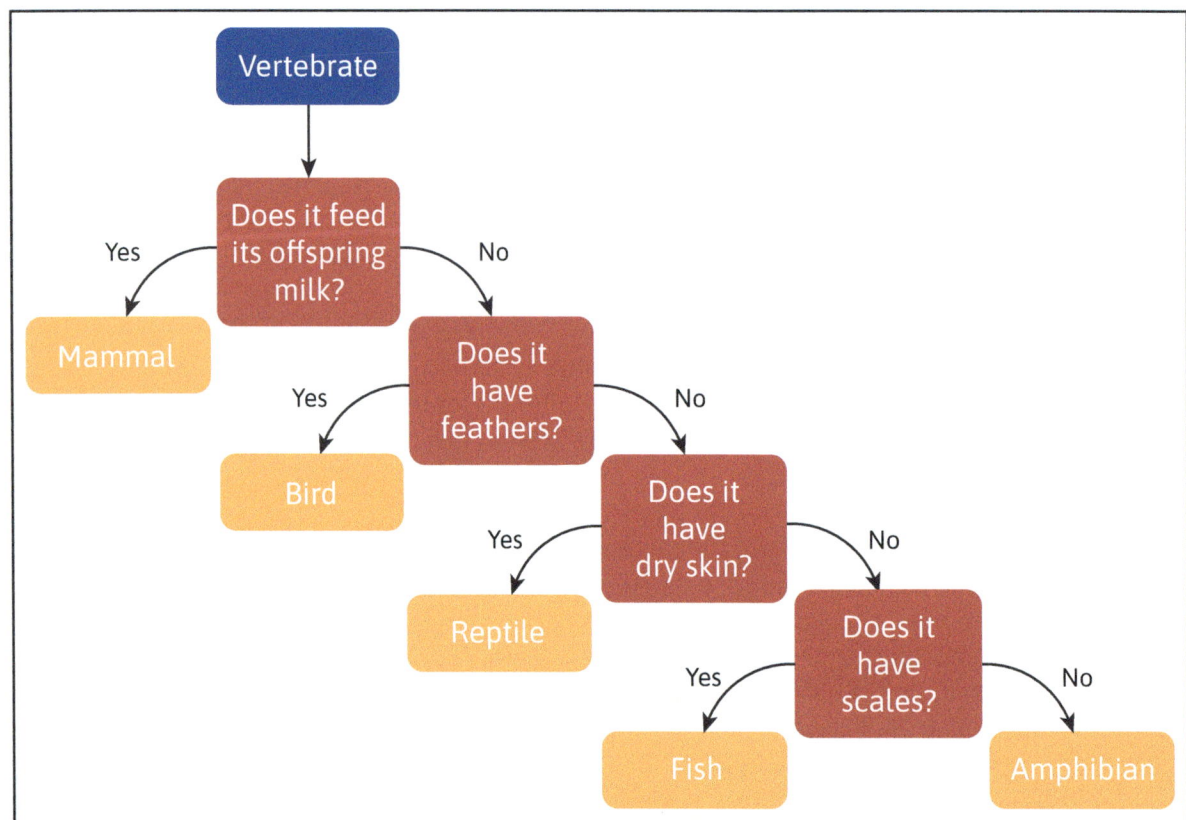

A classification tree.

● Key questions

○ What characteristics can we use to group animals and plants?
The characteristics that are obvious to pupils (e.g. colour, where the organism lives) are often not helpful in classifying animals and plants. In many instances, you will need to show pupils, for example, that insects have six legs and three body parts, whereas a spider has eight legs and a single body part.

○ Can you think of a living thing that might be hard to classify?
Typical examples include whales and dolphins.

○ What characteristics make a living thing fit into a certain group?
This is a particularly useful question to help pupils understand tricky classifications. For example, whales and dolphins are mammals, not fish.

● Common misconceptions

○ Many pupils believe that insects are not animals.
Vertebrates and invertebrates are classified as animals.

○ Many pupils believe that humans are not animals.
Humans are mammals.

○ Many pupils believe that fish are not animals.
Fish are vertebrates.

○ Many pupils believe that whales and dolphins are fish.
This is based on appearance and habitat. Pupils have to understand how dolphins and whales breathe air, give birth to live young and feed their offspring milk.

● Progression

Key Stage	Development of ideas
EYFS	· Pupils start to make sense of their physical world by exploring, observing, and identifying different living things.
KS1	· Pupils should identify, classify and describe their immediate environment and organisms. · Pupilsshould learn about and compare the differences between things that are living, dead, and things that have never been alive.
LKS2	· Pupils should group living things in different ways, learn about and use classification keys to help group, identify and name a variety of living things in their local and wider environment.
UKS2	· Pupils should classify living things into broad groups according to common observable characteristics and based on similarities and differences, including microorganisms, plants and animals.

Vertebrates and invertebrates

The big idea is that vertebrates and invertebrates allow pupils the opportunity to group animals into two distinct groups.

To make the most of this idea, you should focus pupils' attention on the structure and function of the backbone. There are ample opportunities to use their prior knowledge of animals, or images as a stimulation, to group animals in this way.

This is an area that pupils are often really intrigued by as it relates to their own bodies and those of other animals. Using models allows pupils to see the features that we are teaching them, but X-rays and other images are also a good source of visualisation.

The key problem with understanding vertebrates and invertebrates is the superficial similarities between animals, such as snakes and worms, that lead pupils to group them together. The skeleton is unseen and therefore requires careful modelling in order to ensure that pupils create their understanding in a secure way.

Vertebrates   **Invertebrates**

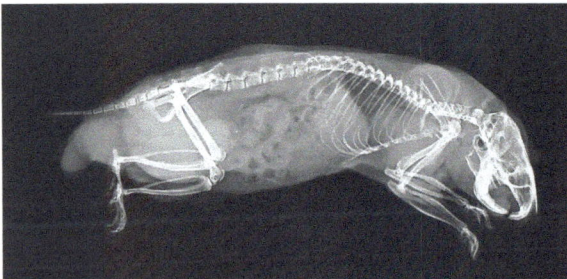

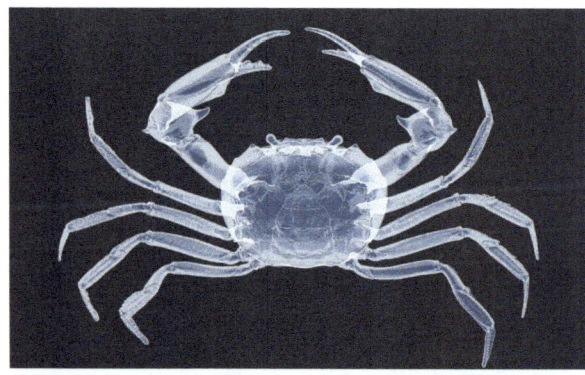

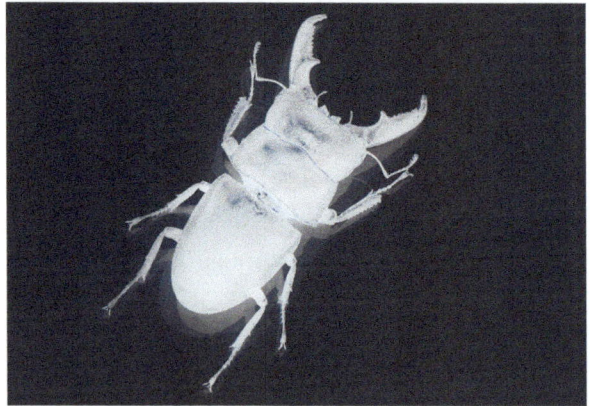

Key questions

What do our vertebrae allow us to do?
As a number of smaller bones make up the vertebra, this allows us to bend rather than be rigid through our backs. The bones also protect the spinal cord, which is key to our nervous system. There are muscles that attach to the bones of the skeleton and allow movement as they contract.

Do all animals have backbones?
No. Some animals have an external skeleton such as a shell (crab), or chitin (insects). These are called exoskeletons. Other animals have skeletons formed from fluids, such as worms, and this is called a hydrostatic skeleton.

Common misconceptions

All animals without legs are invertebrates.
Many pupils hold the misconception that animals that walk (on 2 or 4 legs) are vertebrates, whereas those that do not are invertebrates. Showing images or models of different skeletons can help to amend this view.

Backbones are made from one bone.
Many pupils draw the backbone as one long bone rather than a number of smaller ones. Discussion about what would happen in terms of movement can address this – ask them to bend forwards as if there was only one bone to highlight the case.

Only vertebrates have skeletons.
There are a number of different forms of protection that enable animals such as insects and crustaceans to survive. Exoskeleton is the name given to these, whilst mammals, birds and reptiles have internal skeletons known as endoskeletons.

Progression

Key Stage	Development of ideas
EYFS	· Pupils should explore the natural world around them.
KS1 (ages 5-7)	· Pupils should descibe and compare the structure of a variety of common animals (fish, amphibians, reptiles, birds and mammals, including pets).
KS2 (ages 7-11)	· Pupils will be able to identify that humans and some other animals have skeletons and muscles for support, protection and movement.
KS3 (ages 11-14)	· Pupils shoul learn that the structure and functions of the human skeleton, to include support, protection, movement and making blood cells. Biomechanics – the interaction between skeleton and muscles, including the measurement of force exerted by different muscles.

Mammals

The big idea about mammals is that they are one of the groups of animals, including humans, that inhabit most environments on the planet Earth. They have common characteristics such as maintaining their own body temperature (often referred to as warm-blooded). They usually have fur or hair on their bodies and feed their young, which are usually born live, on milk – although there are, as always, exceptions.

When teaching mammals focus on the differences between these and other groups of animals such as reptiles, birds and fish. The mammals can also be grouped further by characteristics such as what they eat (herbivores, omnivores, carnivores) or where they inhabit.

The difficulty with teaching about mammals is the diversity of this group of animals which live on land and in the sea and also include humans which is often a challenging concept for the pupils. It is best to include a variety of examples of mammals from all habitats.

Key questions

○ **How do mammals maintain their body temperature?**
Mammals generate heat as a product from the reactions in their bodies. They can then regulate this through anatomical adaptations, such as fur and blubber for insulation, as well as behavioural adaptations, such as shivering, sweating or panting and controlling blood flow to the surface of the skin.

○ **How are mammals adapted to their environments?**
Looking at the different features of mammals allows the pupils to learn about adaptations to the environment the mammal inhabits. They can also consider the contribution the mammal makes to the stability of the ecosystem, its place in food webs and the need for conservation of species.

Common misconceptions

O **All mammals live on the land.**
Whilst many different mammals do live on land some live in the water. This includes our largest mammal the Blue Whale. Dolphins, porpoises and manatees are all water dwelling mammals.

O **Mammals never lay eggs.**
There are two exceptions to the rule of mammals giving birth to live young. The first is the platypus which lays eggs that hatch. The second is the echidna. Both of these mammals live in Australia.

O **Humans are not mammals.**
Children often consider humans to be distinct from animals and mammals. Whilst it is important to respect cultural views, from a scientific perspective pupils should learn that humans are also part of the mammal group of animals.

Progression

Key Stage	Development of ideas
EYFS	· Pupils should be able to name and describe some plants and animals that pupils are likely to see, encouraging pupils to recognise familiar plants and animals whilst outside. · Listen to pupils describing and commenting on things that they have seen whilst outside, including plants and animals.
KS1 (ages 5-7)	· Pupils should be able to identify and name a variety of common animals, including fish, amphibians, reptiles, birds and mammals. · Pupils should have the opportunity to describe and compare the structure of a variety of common animals (fish, amphibians, reptiles, birds and mammals, including pets).
LKS2 (ages 7-9)	· Pupils should identify that animals, including humans, need the right types and amount of nutrition, and that they cannot make their own food; they get nutrition from what they eat. · Pupils should be able to identify that humans and some other animals have skeletons and muscles for support, protection and movement. · Pupils should be able to construct and interpret a variety of food chains, identifying producers, predators and prey.
UKS2 (ages 9-11)	· Pupils should be able to describe the changes as humans develop to old age. · Pupils should describe how living things are classified into broad groups according to common observable characteristics and based on similarities and differences, including microorganisms, plants and animals. · Pupils should be able to give reasons for classifying plants and animals based on specific characteristics.
KS3 (ages 11-14)	· Pupils should be able to describe the variation between species and between individuals of the same species, meaning that some organisms compete more successfully, which can drive natural selection. · Pupils should be able to identify changes in the environment, which may leave individuals within a species, and some entire species, less well adapted to compete successfully and reproduce, which in turn may lead to extinction. · Pupils should know the importance of maintaining biodiversity and the use of gene banks to preserve hereditary material.

Insects

The big idea is that insects play a key role in the ecosystem and are extremely varied in their appearance and roles.

To make the most of this idea you should focus on the characteristics of insects. These all have body segments – the head, thorax and abdomen. The head contains the insect's sensory organs and mouthparts, while the thorax is where the wings and legs are attached. The abdomen contains the insect's digestive and reproductive organs. Insects have six legs, which are attached to the thorax. The legs are used for walking, climbing, jumping and, sometimes, swimming.

Insects also have an exoskeleton, which is a hard outer covering that provides support and protection. The exoskeleton is made of a substance called chitin, and must be shed periodically in a process called moulting to allow for growth.

Most, but not all, adult insects have wings. Insects have two pairs of wings, which are attached to the thorax. The wings are used for flight, as well as for display and communication in some species.

Linking with life cycles, many insects undergo metamorphosis, which is a process of transformation from a larval form to an adult form. There are two main types of metamorphosis: incomplete metamorphosis, in which the insect goes through several stages of development without a pupal stage, and complete metamorphosis, in which the insect goes through four distinct stages: egg, larva, pupa, and adult.

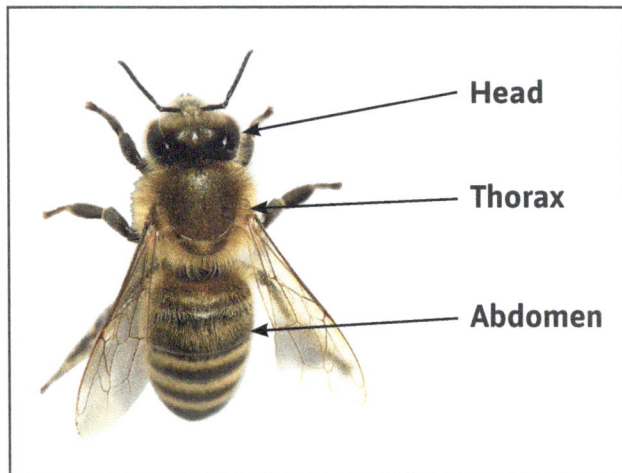

Key questions

What are the benefits of insects in the environment?
Insects are key pollinators, ensuring that pollen is transferred from plant to plant so that they can reproduce. Insects also play an important part in decomposition, which recycles nutrients in the environment. They are a good source of food for many birds, mammals and reptiles, so they have an important role in maintaining stable ecosystems.

○ **Do all insects bite?**
Insects that commonly bite or sting include mosquitoes, bees, wasps, hornets, ants and some types of flies. These insects use their mouthparts or stingers to defend themselves, or to feed on blood or other substances. However, many other insects do not bite or sting humans. For example, many species of butterflies, moths, and beetles do not have the ability to bite or sting, and rely on other methods of defence such as camouflage or toxic chemicals.

● Common misconceptions

○ **Insects and bugs are the same.**
The terms 'bug' and 'insect' are often used interchangeably; however, bugs are actually a sub-category of insects.

○ **Spiders and other invertebrates are insects.**
Insects in their adult form have three body parts and six legs. Spiders and many other invertebrates are not classified as insects.

○ **Insects are not animals.**
Insects are a class within the phylum of *Arthropoda*, which is a group of invertebrate animals.

○ **All insects are pests.**
While some insects can be pests, not all insects are harmful to humans. In fact, many insects are beneficial, such as those that control pest populations or pollinate crops.

● Progression

Key Stage	Development of ideas
EYFS	· Pupils should use scientific vocabulary when talking about the parts of a flower or an insect, or different types of rocks. · Help pupils to come up with their own ideas and explanations. *Suggestion: you could look together at woodlice and caterpillars outdoors with the magnifying app on a tablet. You could ask: 'What's similar about caterpillars and other insects?' You could use and explain terms such as 'antennae' and 'thorax'.*
KS1 (ages 5-7)	· Pupils should be able to identify and name a variety of insects in their habitats, including microhabitats.
LKS2 (ages 7-9)	· Pupils should learn about and use classification keys to help group, identify and name a variety of insects in their local and wider environment.
UKS2 (ages 9-11)	· Pupils should be able to describe the life cycles of various insects and compare them to other categories of animal.
KS3 (ages 11-14)	· Pupils should understand how organisms are grouped, using the Linnaean system (which includes the classification of insects). · Pupils hould understand the principles of ecology, including the interdependence of organisms (how insects interact with their environment and other organisms). · Pupils should learn about genetics and evolution, including natural selection and selective breeding (potentially studying insects such as silkworms and honey bees as examples).

Microorganisms

The big idea of microorganisms is that they are microscopic and the most abundant life forms on Earth, found in every ecosystem.

To make the most of this idea, pupils need to get a clear understanding of the size, abundance and diversity of microorganisms on Earth. They understand the roles that microorganisms play in different habitats, including our bodies.

The key problem with microorganisms is that they can't be seen using equipment that a school has access to. Visualising the size of microorganisms in comparison to known objects is very challenging.

Understanding their abundance and diversity compared to other animals is an almost impossible concept for pupils. You can use analogies to give a sense of their size and abundance – millions of bacteria would fit on the head of a pin.

Microorganisms play a crucial role in many natural and artificial processes – we literally wouldn't be here if it wasn't for them.

Microorganisms are also known as microbes.

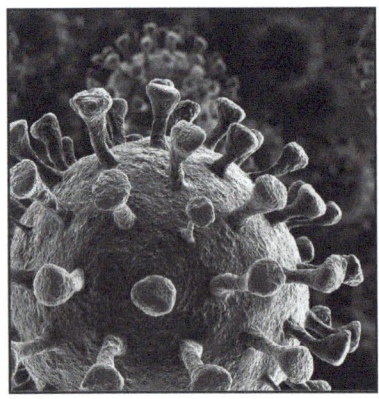 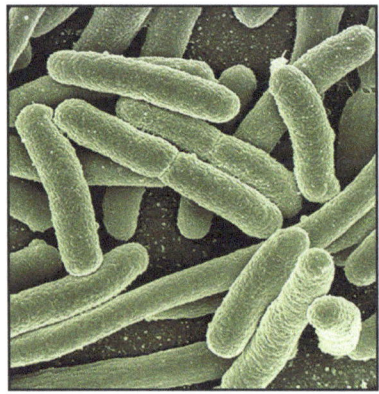 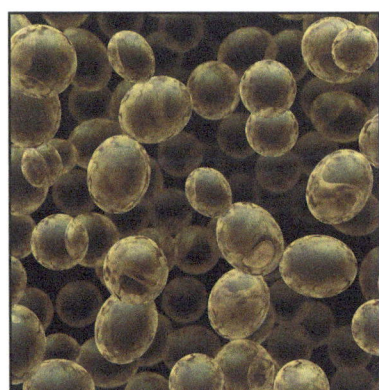

Virus (Coronavirus)   **Bacteria (*E. Coli*)**   **Fungi (yeast)**

● Key questions

○ **What are the different types of microorganism?**
The main types of microorganism are bacteria (e.g. *E.coli*), viruses (e.g. Coronavirus), fungi (e.g. yeast) and algae (e.g. green algae on a pond surface).

○ **What is the difference between bacteria and viruses?**
Bacteria are free-living organisms capable of reproduction in almost any environment. Viruses need a host cell to reproduce; their reproduction causes the death of the cell that they are using. Bacteria are much larger and more complex than viruses, which are really simple (a protein capsule round a piece of genetic material; usually *DNA*).

○ **Are all microorganisms harmful?**
No. Most microorganisms are not harmful to humans and many help us survive. Some break down food as we digest it; some take atmospheric nitrogen from the air and turn it into nitrates that are essential for plants to grow; yeasts and bacteria are used in fermentation food preparation processes (e.g. for cheese and yoghurt), and they are also present in the study of genetics and diseases. They are used for antibiotic production, to clean up oil spills and to process other industrial waste – some can literally digest plastic!

● Common misconceptions

○ **All microorganisms are bad for you and cause disease.**
Very few bacteria are 'pathogens', disease-causing; most of them are essential for life. Bacteria aid digestion, help us to fight infection and decompose dead organic matter, returning nutrients to the soil.

○ **If I am ill, I need antibiotics to make me better.**
Most common illnesses, colds and flus, are caused by viruses. So, taking antibiotics won't have any effect. In the long term, taking antibiotics has a negative effect on the bacteria that are good for you and can lower your immune system.

○ **Bacteria and other microorganisms are not living things.**
Bacteria are living things that are made of a single cell. They need nutrients, can reproduce, move, grow and sense the environment around them.

● Progression

Key Stage	Development of ideas
EYFS	· Pupils should understand the key features of the life cycle of a plant and an animal.
KS1 (ages 5-7)	· Pupils should explore and compare the differences between things that are living, dead, and things that have never been alive.
LKS2 (ages 7-9)	· Pupils should be able to recognise that living things can be grouped in a variety of ways.
UKS2 (ages 9-11)	· Pupils should be able to describe how living things are classified into broad groups according to common observable characteristics and based on similarities and differences, including microorganisms.
KS3 (ages 11-14)	· Pupils should be taught about cells as the fundamental unit of living organisms, including how to observe, interpret and record cell structure using a light microscope. · Pupils should also learn about the structural adaptations of some unicellular organisms and the importance of bacteria in the human digestive system.

Food chains and webs

The big idea of food chains and webs is to ensure that pupils understand the interdependence of plants and animals, which creates an ecosystem.

To make the most of this idea, pupils need to see how plants and animals are interdependent. This can be achieved through creating food chains and food webs (see images below). In addition, pupils need to learn about what happens when a plant or animal is removed from an ecosystem and how this impacts on the other living things.

The key problem with exploring the interdependence of ecosystems through using food chains and food webs is that it can be hard to consider the wider impact. The linear model of a food chain doesn't consider the complexity of the interdependence of an ecosystem and can appear to end with the predator at the 'top' of a food chain.

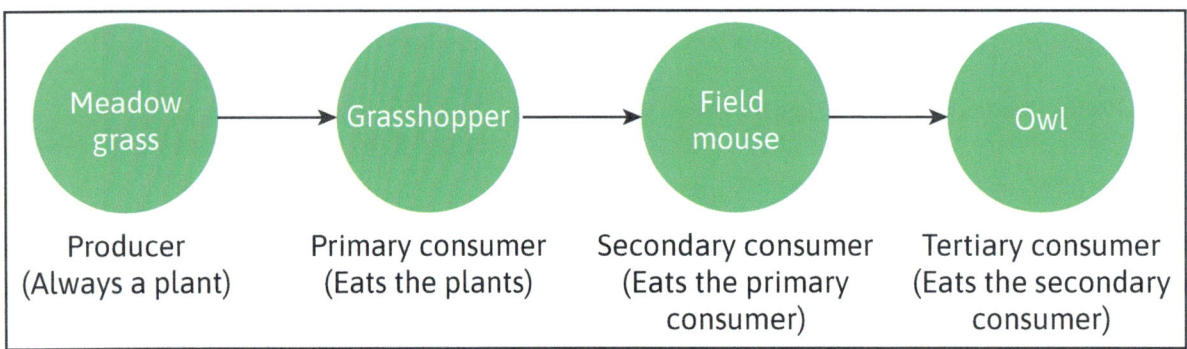

A simple food chain

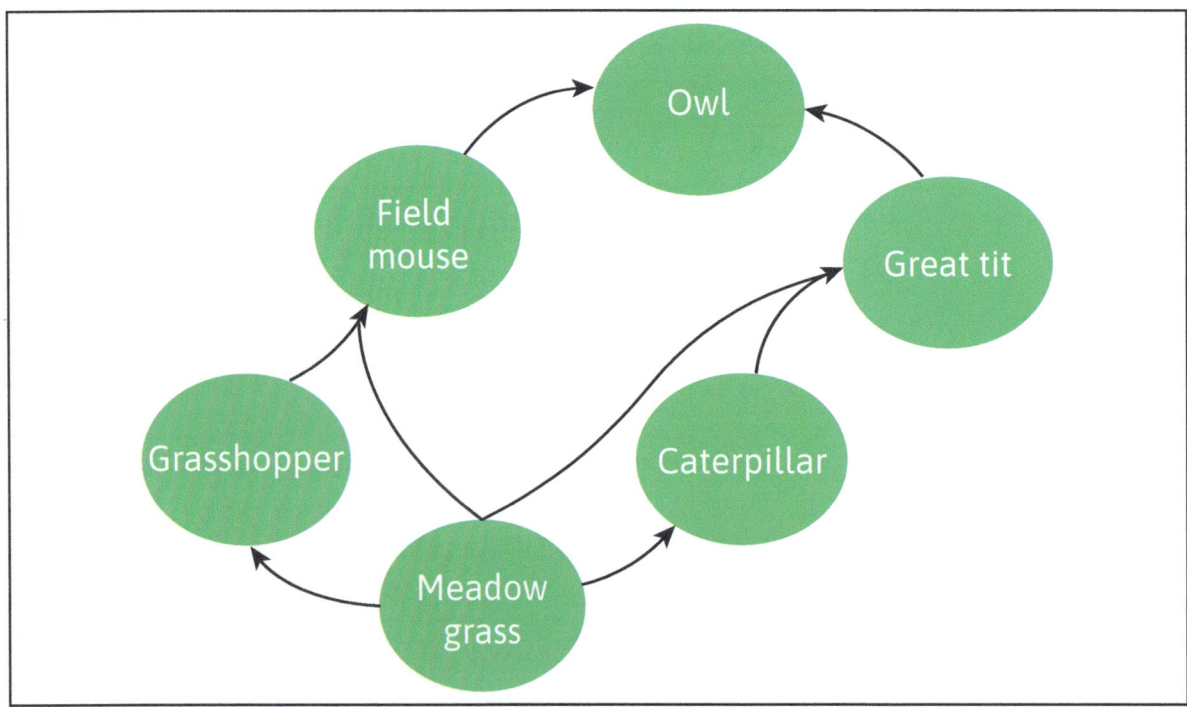

A simple food web

Key questions

○ **What do animals eat in a habitat?**

○ **Can you draw a food chain or web based on this ecosystem?**

○ **Can you name the producers, predators and prey within a habitat?**

Common misconceptions

○ **Pupils often think that the arrows in a food chain mean 'eats'.**
The arrows show the direction in which the food (carbohydrates and nutrients) travel.

○ **Pupils often think that the death of one of the parts of a food chain or web is independent, or has limited consequences on the rest of the chain.**
In fact, the death of one organism in the food chain often has significant impact on the whole chain – in both directions.

○ **There is always plenty of food for wild animals.**
Food is almost always limited for wild animals, which has an impact on their populations.

Progression

Key Stage	Development of ideas
EYFS	· Pupils should be able to match animals with the different foods that they eat.
KS1 (ages 5-7)	· Pupils should be able to identify and name a variety of common animals that are carnivores, herbivores and omnivores. · Pupils should describe how animals obtain their food from plants and other animals, using the idea of a simple food chain, and identify and name different sources of food.
KS2 (ages 7-11)	· Pupils should be able to identify that animals, including humans, need the right types and amount of nutrition, and that they cannot make their own food – they get nutrition from what they eat. · Pupils should construct and interpret a variety of food chains, identifying producers, predators and prey.
KS3 (ages 11-14)	· Pupils should be able to identify and describe different trophic levels within a food chain, such as producers, primary consumers, secondary consumers, and tertiary consumers. · Pupils should understand the role of decomposers in breaking down dead organisms and recycling nutrients back into the ecosystem. Pupil should recognise that energy is transferred along food chains and that the efficiency of this transfer is limited, resulting in a reduction of available energy at each trophic level. · Pupils should be able to construct and interpret food webs, which are complex networks of interconnected food chains within an ecosystem. · Pupils should understand the importance of biodiversity and the potential impact of changes in an ecosystem on food chains and food webs, including the consequences of species extinction or introduction of new species.

Life cycles

The big idea is that animals and plants have life cycles, which go through various stages. The stages depend on the type of organism.

To make the most of this idea, you should focus pupils on the broad stages that different plants and animals go through – highlighting the differences between mammals, which give birth to live young (with the exceptions of the duck-billed platypus and echidnas), and birds and reptiles, which generally lay eggs. There are many examples that can be observed within the classroom, such as seed growth, frog spawn in a local pond, or caterpillars metamorphosing into butterflies.

The key problem with life cycles is the understanding in young pupils of the correct order for the sequence and application of this to their own lives, which may also be emotional for them.

Key questions

O **Do all plants and animals have life cycles?**
Although individual plants and animals will have different life cycles, they have central components of start of life, reproduction and death.

O **What would happen if a species of animal or plant never reproduced?**
Eventually, when every specimen of that species had died, the species would be extinct.

O **Do any animals or plants live forever?**
Some plants and animals can live a surprisingly long time (some trees are hundreds of years old). Nevertheless, we have never found a species that can live forever.

Common misconceptions

○ **Humans don't have a life cycle.**
Sometimes the life cycle concept is not applied to humans, but humans, like all living organisms, have a life cycle that includes birth, growth, reproduction, ageing and death.

○ **Plants don't have life cycles.**
People often overlook plants when thinking about life cycles, but plants also have complex life stages, including germination, growth, flowering, seed production and death. The process may differ significantly between various types of plants.

○ **Metamorphosis occurs in all insects.**
While many insects undergo metamorphosis (like butterflies), not all insects experience this transformation. Some insects, like silverfish, have a life cycle without metamorphic stages.

○ **Birds grow in the egg in the same way that mammals grow in the womb.**
Although both birds and mammals start as embryos, the development process and conditions are quite different. Bird embryos develop in eggs outside the mother's body and receive nourishment from the yolk, while mammalian embryos develop inside the mother and receive nourishment from her body.

○ **All mammals give live birth.**
Most mammals give birth to live young, but there are exceptions, such as monotremes (e.g. platypuses and echidnas), which lay eggs.

Progression

Key Stage	Development of ideas
EYFS	· Help pupils to care for animals and take part in first-hand scientific explorations of animal life cycles, such as caterpillars or chick eggs.
KS1 (ages 5-7)	· Pupils should compare the differences between things that are living, dead, and things that have never been alive.
LKS2 (ages 7-9)	· Pupils should use classification keys to help group, identify and name a variety of living things in their local and wider environment. · Pupils should recognise that environments can change and that this can sometimes pose dangers to living things.
UKS2 (ages 7-9)	· Pupils should be able to describe the differences in the life cycles of a mammal, an amphibian, an insect and a bird. · Pupils should be able to describe the life process of reproduction in some plants and animals. · Pupils should be able to describe the changes as humans develop to old age.
KS3 (ages 11-14)	· Pupils should be taught about reproduction in humans (as an example of a mammal), including the structure and function of the male and female reproductive systems, menstrual cycle (without details of hormones), gametes, fertilisation, gestation and birth, to include the effect of maternal lifestyle on the foetus through the placenta. · Pupils should also learn about reproduction in plants, including flower structure, wind and insect pollination, fertilisation, seed and fruit formation and dispersal, including quantitative investigation of some dispersal mechanisms.

Leaves and photosynthesis

The big idea of leaves is that they use sunlight, carbon dioxide and water to produce food for plants (sugars). To make the most of leaves, pupils need to observe a variety of different leaves, including those growing on plants, and see how these change over the course of a year. To understand photosynthesis, pupils will need clear models, possibly diagrams, to explain the process.

The key problem with photosynthesis is that it is an abstract concept that is very difficult to observe. Pupils need to understand the following (albeit superficially) before they can understand photosynthesis:

- carbon dioxide is a gas in the air;
- oxygen is a gas in the air produced by photosynthesis;
- plants make their own food in their leaves; and
- photosynthesis needs water taken in by the roots and transported to the leaves. Sunlight is needed to cause the transformation of water and carbon dioxide into sugar (the food) and oxygen.

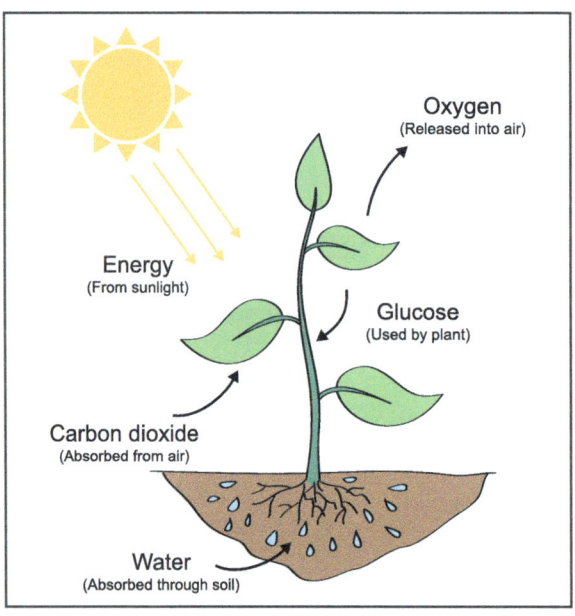

Key questions

○ **Can you describe what a leaf looks like and how it feels?**
This encourages pupils to use their senses to observe and describe leaves.

○ **Why do you think leaves are important for a plant?**
The key function of a leaf is to produce food (sugars) for the plant by photosynthesis.

○ **What would happen if a plant didn't have any leaves?**
Without leaves, most plants cannot make food and they will die.

O **Have you noticed that leaves look different on different types of plants? Why do you think this might be?**
This question helps pupils to recognise that plants, including their leaves, come in many shapes and sizes, and it encourages them to think about why this might be (adaptations may include prickles (e.g. holly) to reduce predation, succulent leaves to store water (e.g. Aloe Vera), and variegated leaves (to trick insects into believing that the leaf has already been eaten).

● Common misconceptions

O **Plants 'eat' food and this food comes from the soil via the roots.**
Plants get nutrients from the soil (including nitrogen, phosphorus and potassium), but these are not described as 'food'. Plants make their own food (sugars) through photosynthesis, which occurs in the leaves.

O **You cannot eat leaves.**
Some pupils will not believe that vegetables such as lettuce and spinach are leaves. Teachers need to provide pupils with examples of leaves that are edible, whilst reminding pupils that not all leaves are safe to eat and that they must always check with an adult first.

O **Plants make oxygen so that animals including humans can breathe.**
Oxygen is a by-product of photosynthesis. Plants do not make oxygen for us to breathe – we only take advantage of oxygen as a natural waste product of photosynthesis.

● Progression

Key Stage	Development of ideas
EYFS	· Encourage and support pupils to observe and ask questions about the natural world around them, including plants. They may notice changes in plants and trees throughout the year, but they won't learn about photosynthesis at this stage.
KS1 (ages 5-7)	· Pupils should identify and name a variety of common wild and garden plants. They should understand the basic structure of a variety of common flowering plants, including trees, which would involve the identification of leaves. However, photosynthesis is not introduced at this stage.
LKS2 (ages 7-9)	· Pupils should identify and describe the functions of different parts of flowering plants: roots, stem/trunk, leaves and flowers. This would include an understanding of the role of leaves in plants' life processes, including their role in the transport of water, although photosynthesis is still not explicitly taught.
UKS2 (ages 9-11)	· Pupils should be introduced to photosynthesis and understand it as a process vital for the life of plants and the development of life on Earth. They should learn that plants make their own food in their leaves, using carbon dioxide, water and sunlight. They may learn that oxygen is a by-product of photosynthesis.
KS3 (ages 11-14)	· Pupils should deepen their understanding of photosynthesis as a key biological process. They should learn about the reactants in, and products of, photosynthesis, and why it is important in the life processes of plants. They should understand the role of the leaf in photosynthesis, including adaptations for this process.

Flowers

The big idea is that flowers are a key part of a plant's survival as their means of reproduction and/or pollination.

To make the most of this idea, you should focus pupils' attention on the different parts of a flower. Even at a very young age, children can observe the different textures, colours and parts that flowers have.

The examples used should be of commonly recognised flowers such as those found in the school grounds – dandelions, daffodils and daisies perhaps – as well as those found on vegetables (broccoli) and grasses. This challenges the idea that all flowers are the same.

The key problem with teaching about flowers is that they are – like most plants topics – taken very much for granted. Their complexities are often overlooked. It is challenging for pupils to recognise the role that they play without a real understanding of plant reproduction.

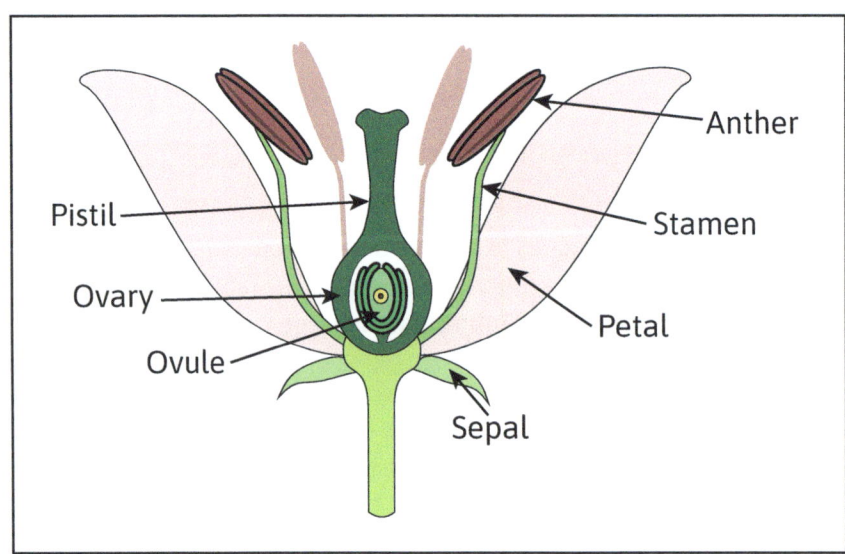

Key questions

O Do all plants flower?
There are different groups of plants, some of which are flowering and some are non-flowering.

O Are all flowers the same?
No. Many flowers have the same parts that can be observed, but they don't all look exactly the same, or have the same visible parts.

O What is the purpose of a flower?
Flowers are part of a plant's reproductive cycle. Their purpose might be to attract insects, or to allow wind pollination.

Common misconceptions

O Flowers are not parts of the plant.
Young pupils will sometimes refer to flowers and plants rather than seeing the flower as part of the plant (or part of the plant life cycle).

O Trees do not flower.
The preconception of what a flower looks like challenges the pupils in terms of 'seeing' other flowers. This is why using a range of examples is important.

O Flowers are always colourful.
Due to representation in books and first-hand experiences with flowers, pupils will consider that they are always bright and colourful. Again, this demonstrates the need for a good range of examples.

Progression

Key Stage	Development of ideas
EYFS	· Pupils should use scientific vocabulary when talking about the parts of a flower.
KS1 (ages 5-7)	· Pupils should be able to identify and describe the basic structure of a variety of common flowering plants, including trees.
LKS2 (ages 7-9)	· Pupils should identify and describe the functions of different parts of flowers. · They should explore the part that flowers play in the life cycle of flowering plants, including pollination, seed formation and seed dispersal.
UKS2 (ages 9-11)	· Pupils should be able to describe how living things are classified into broad groups according to common observable characteristics and based on similarities and differences, including microorganisms, plants and animals (*can group plants based on flowering/non-flowering*).
KS3 (ages 11-14)	· Pupils should learn about reproduction in plants, including flower structure, wind and insect pollination, fertilisation, seed and fruit formation and dispersal, including quantitative investigation of some dispersal mechanisms.

Pollination

The big idea of pollination is that pollen, which is produced by the male part of the flower, is transferred to the female part of another flower. This can be done by insects or by the wind. Pollination only occurs in flowering plants that need two parent plants in order to reproduce sexually.

To make the most of the topic, it would be good to look at a variety of flowering plants, including grasses, to observe the similarities and differences. Pupils should also recognise the function of the flower in attracting pollinators, and that wind-pollinated plants have small flowers that are not brightly coloured. Doing a flower dissection is a really good way to help pupils to identify the different parts of the flower and their functions.

The key problem with pollination is that pupils cannot easily see pollination in action. At the right time of year, pupils can go outside to observe bees going from one flower to another. Then you could replicate what they have observed in more detail by doing a role play model of pollination so that pupils get the idea of pollen moving from one flower to another. Another thing to consider is that pollen itself is hard to see with the naked eye and, therefore, investing in a magnifier for pupils to see it enlarged is a good idea.

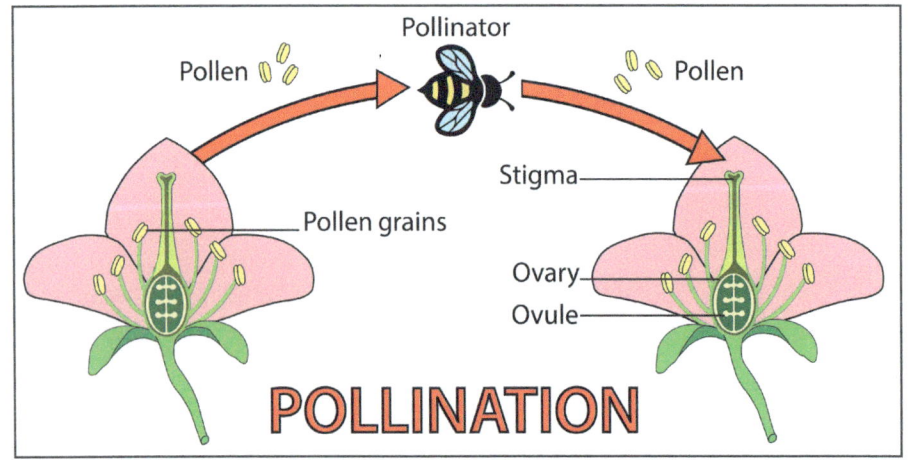

Insects carry pollen grains from an anther to a stigma.

Key questions

○ **What is pollination?**
Pollination is the transfer of pollen from the anther of one flower to the stigma on another flower.

○ **Are only bees pollinators?**
No. Other animals such as hummingbirds, butterflies and even some bats are pollinators.

○ **What are the two methods of pollination in plants?**
The two methods are by insect (or other animal) and by wind.

○ **What is the function of the flower?**
To attract pollinators with brightly coloured petals and scent.

Common misconceptions

○ **Seed dispersal and pollination are not the same.**
These are two different processes. Pollination is where pollen is delivered to a stigma. Seed dispersal happens later when the fertilised seeds are carried away from the plant.

○ **Pollination and fertilisation are not the same.**
Pollination is the process where pollen is moved from one plant to another. Fertilisation is when pollen and ovule join.

○ **Insects pollinate plants deliberately.**
The insect is an unwitting part of the pollination process. While getting nectar, the insects brush against the pollen when they climb over the flower.

○ **Only bees pollinate flowers.**
Other insects and even humming birds and bats also pollinate flowers. Many flowers are also pollinated by the wind.

Progression

Key Stage	Development of ideas
EYFS	· Pupils should explore the natural world around them, making observations and drawing pictures of animals and plants. · Pupils should learn the names of common flowering plants and pollinators.
KS1 (ages 5-7)	· Pupils should identify and name a variety of common wild and garden plants, including deciduous and evergreen trees. · Pupils should identify and describe the basic structure of a variety of common flowering plants, including trees. · Pupils should observe and describe how seeds and bulbs grow into mature plants. · Pupils should understand that plants need water, light and a suitable temperature to grow and stay healthy.
LKS2 (ages 7-9)	· Pupils should explore the part that flowers play in the life cycle of flowering plants, including pollination, seed formation and seed dispersal. · Pupils should be introduced to the relationship between structure and function: flowers for reproduction.
UKS2 (ages 9-11)	· Pupils should be able to describe the life process of reproduction in some plants and animals. · Pupils should observe life cycle changes in a variety of living things, for example, plants in the vegetable garden or flower border. · Pupils should find out about different types of reproduction, including sexual and asexual reproduction in plants.
KS3 (ages 11-14)	Reproduction: ·Pupils should learn about reproduction in plants, including flower structure, wind and insect pollination, fertilisation, seed and fruit formation and dispersal, including quantitative investigation of some dispersal mechanisms; ·Pupils should learn about interactions and interdependencies. Relationships in an ecosystem: ·Pupils should learn about the interdependence of organisms in an ecosystem, including food webs and insect-pollinated crops; ·Pupils should learn about the importance of plant reproduction through insect pollination in human food security.

Fertilisation

The big idea of fertilisation is that it happens when the ovule and pollen grain join together in the ovary. The final product of this process is the formation of embryos in a seed.

To make the most of the topic of fertilisation, pupils should understand that flowering plant life cycles need two flowers for cross-pollination and fertilisation; this is called sexual reproduction. The male pollen grain needs to join with the female ovule. In Upper Key Stage 2 (ages 9-11), pupils may also look at asexual reproduction, which only needs one parent plant. The parent plant makes an exact copy of itself. Some methods of asexual reproduction include runners (e.g. spider plants), tubers (e.g. potatoes) and bulbs (e.g. garlic).

The key problem with fertilisation is that it is confused with pollination. Pollination, as a process, must happen first, as pollen is transferred from one plant to another, in order for fertilisation to take place. It is hard to show fertilisation to pupils, which is why the step often gets missed. Use of video clips can help support the learning of this step. It is also worth considering that some plants can reproduce both sexually and asexually; for example, strawberries produce small white flowers and runners, and daffodils produce brightly coloured flowers and split their bulbs. This gives them an even better chance of producing another generation.

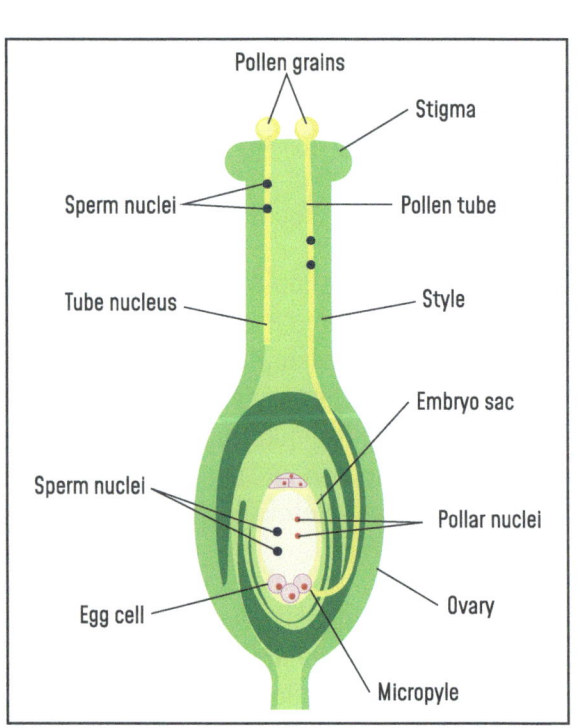

Diagram showing pollen fertilising an ovule.

Key questions

○ **What parts of the flower are involved in fertilisation?**
Pollen and an ovule in the ovary.

○ **What is fertilisation?**
The joining of the pollen and the ovule, which will result in a seed.

○ **What are the 3 key steps in fertilisation?**
1. Pollen grain lands on the stigma.
2. Pollen tube is grown.
3. Pollen and ovule join in the ovary.

Common misconceptions

O Children may incorrectly think that flowers are just there for decoration, rather than an important part of the plant reproductive system.

O Children may incorrectly think that all plants need animals in order for pollination to happen. Some are wind-pollinated.

O Some pupils may incorrectly think that:
- all plants start out as seeds (some plants reproduce asexually, such as strawberries using 'runners');
- all plants have flowers;
- plants that grow from bulbs do not have seeds; and
- seeds are not alive.

Progression

Key Stage	Development of ideas
EYFS	· Pupil should have the opportunity to explore the natural world around them, making observations and drawing pictures of animals and plants.
KS1 (ages 5-7)	· Pupil should be able to identify and name a variety of common wild and garden plants, including deciduous and evergreen trees. · Pupils should be able to identify and describe the basic structure of a variety of common flowering plants, including trees. · Pupils should observe and describe how seeds and bulbs grow into mature plants. · Pupils should find out and describe how plants need water, light and a suitable temperature to grow and stay healthy.
LKS2 (ages 7-9)	· Pupils should learn the part that flowers play in the life cycle of flowering plants, including pollination, seed formation and seed dispersal. · Pupils should be introduced to the relationship between structure and function: flowers for reproduction.
UKS2 (ages 9-11)	· Pupils should be able to describe the life process of reproduction in some plants and animals. · Pupils should observe life cycle changes in a variety of living things, for example, plants in the vegetable garden or flower border. · Pupils should find out about different types of reproduction, including sexual and asexual reproduction in plants.
KS3 (ages 11-14)	Reproduction: ·Pupils should learn about reproduction in plants, including flower structure, wind and insect pollination, fertilisation, seed and fruit formation and dispersal, including quantitative investigation of some dispersal mechanisms; ·Pupils should learn about interactions and interdependencies. Relationships in an ecosystem: ·Pupils should learn about the interdependence of organisms in an ecosystem, including food webs and insect-pollinated crops; ·Pupils should learn about the importance of plant reproduction through insect pollination in human food security.

Seed dispersal

The big idea of seed dispersal is that seeds are scattered away from the parent plant. This is so they are not in competition with the parent plant for light, space, nutrients and water. The seeds that land on suitable ground will grow into new plants. There are five key methods of seed dispersal: wind, water, animal hair, animal eating and explosion.

To make the most of seed dispersal, you should take the time to go outside and look at real seeds being dispersed. For wind dispersal, you could observe the process in autumn with sycamore seeds or, in summer, with dandelion seeds. To observe fruit dispersal, you have black berries and rose hips in the autumn, or apples and other fruit on trees in the summer. This is where animals eat the fruit (seeds and all) and excrete them (poo them out).

The key problem with seed dispersal is that you may not have access to a variety of seed types and their different dispersal methods. Therefore, planning in advance is important so that seeds can be collected. It is important that we don't just talk about how fruit seeds are dispersed, or how wind dispersal happens (these are the two easier ones to tackle in a class). Other seeds to consider are: burdocks and goosegrass with hooks (animal fur), poppy seed heads (shaking), peas in their pods (explosion) and coconuts (water – most pupils will think coconuts will sink because of their size, but they float so can be dispersed).

Winged seed – wind dispersal

Hooks and barbs – animal dispersal

Seeds in pods – explosion dispersal

Fibrous seed – water dispersal

● Key questions

○ **Why are seeds dispersed?**
Seeds are dispersed so that new plants are not in competition with the parent plant for water, space, light and nutrients.

○ **What are the methods of seed dispersal?**
The main methods of seed dispersal are water, wind, animal eating, animal fur (hitch-hiking) and explosion.

○ **What are the stages of a plant life cycle?**
The stages are germination, growth, flowering, pollination, fertilisation, seed dispersal.

Common misconceptions

○ **All seeds need light to germinate.**
While some seeds require light, many germinate just fine in complete darkness. Light can be helpful but isn't essential for all.

○ **Seeds are dead.**
Seeds are actually alive, just dormant and waiting for the right conditions to germinate. They contain a living embryo and stored food sources.

○ **Bigger seeds produce bigger plants.**
Seed size doesn't necessarily correlate to plant size. Smaller seeds can produce large plants and vice versa. Factors like genetics and growing conditions play a bigger role.

Progression

Key Stage	Development of ideas
EYFS	· Pupil should explore the natural world around them, making observations and drawing pictures of animals and plants.
KS1 (ages 5-7)	· Pupils should be able to identify and name a variety of common wild and garden plants, including deciduous and evergreen trees. · Pupils should be able to identify and describe the basic structure of a variety of common flowering plants, including trees. · Pupils should have opportunity to observe and describe how seeds and bulbs grow into mature plants. · Pupils should find out and describe how plants need water, light and a suitable temperature to grow and stay healthy.
LKS2 (ages 7-9)	· Pupils should learn the part that flowers play in the life cycle of flowering plants, including pollination, seed formation and seed dispersal. · Pupils should be introduced to the relationship between structure and function: flowers for reproduction.
UKS2 (ages 9-11)	· Pupils should be able to describe the life process of reproduction in some plants and animals. · Pupils should observe life cycle changes in a variety of living things: for example, plants in the vegetable garden or flower border. · Pupils should find out about different types of reproduction, including sexual and asexual reproduction in plants.
KS3 (ages 11-14)	· Pupils should learn about reproduction in plants, including flower structure, wind and insect pollination, fertilisation, seed and fruit formation and dispersal, including quantitative investigation of some dispersal mechanisms. · Puils should learn about interdependence of organisms in an ecosystem, including food webs and insect pollinated crops and the importance of plant reproduction through insect pollination in human food security.

Stems

The big idea of stems is that they contain the transport system for plants. Stems transport water and minerals from the roots to the leaves and flowers. They provide support and keep the plant standing upright. The stem also acts as a store for water and minerals.

To make the most of teaching stems, teachers will need to provide many different examples of stems from trees, flowers and shrubs (simplified diagrams are useful, but pupils need to see a wide variety of different real stems). Teachers should show the pupils edible stems such as celery and conduct experiments to show the passage of water and nutrients through the stem by putting them in coloured water for a few days (celery and carnations work well for this). It would be useful to have some potted plants in the classroom that the pupils can look after and, if the school has a nature area or a school garden, to observe stems growing outdoors. Children can use digital microscopes and hand lenses to look at the phloem and xylem tubes in cross-sections of cut stems.

The key problem with stems is timing. Firstly, you need time in order to grow the plants ready for observation and experiments. If growing plants from seed (which is the most economical way), these need to be planted months in advance and kept indoors, which is not always possible. Plants and cut flowers can be purchased on the day of lessons, but this can be quite expensive. Stems can be observed outside at most times of year, but are best studied in the autumn and summer because that is when some plants are changing (growing and becoming dormant). Like leaves, it is important to look at stems during every school term in order to observe any differences and avoid misconceptions. When bringing plants and seeds into the classroom, teachers must be aware of any allergies the pupils might have.

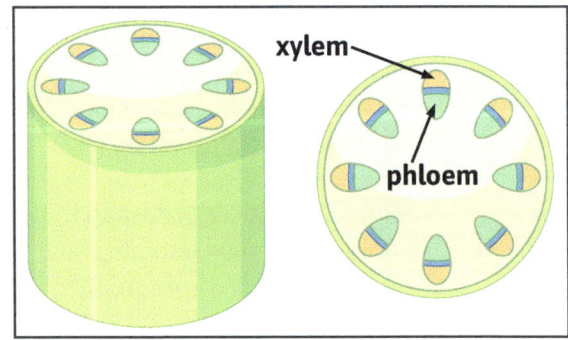

A cross-section of a stem showing the phloem and xylem.

Key questions

○ **What are the functions of stems?**
To support the plant, provide transport and storage of water and nutrients.

○ **Can plants survive without stems?**
No, without stems, the plant cannot transport water and nutrients, so the plant will die. However, some stems will regenerate when cut, for example coppiced trees.

○ **How do stems work?**
Stems contain two different types of tube, which conduct materials up and down the plant. The tubes that carry water up the stem are called xylem. The other tubes (called phloem) carry sugar from the leaves to the rest of the plant.

○ **Which stems do we eat?**
We eat a variety of vegetable stems such as celery, rhubarb and asparagus.

Common misconceptions

○ **All plants have stems.**
Some plants called *Bryophytes*, such as moss and liverworts, have no roots, leaves or stems. They are flowerless plants that grow in clumps.

○ **Stems and trunks are different.**
They are the same. The stem of a tree is called its trunk. The stem often divides into smaller branches at the top of the plant.

○ **Plants drink water through their stems.**
Plants do not 'drink' like animals do. Water and minerals are drawn up the xylem inside the stem from the roots all the way up to the leaves. The xylem acts like a drinking straw, sucking water up from the roots.

○ **Stems only transport water, nutrients and food to other parts of the plant.**
No. Stems have other functions: they keep the plant upright and support the leaves and flowers. They also act as a store for minerals and nutrients.

○ **Stems only grow above ground.**
No. Some plants have stems that grow under the ground, such as garlic or onions. Other stems grow along the ground, for example sweet potato and strawberry plants.

○ **Stems are always straight.**
Some plant stems grow in spirals, such as sweet peas and beans. Others form tendrils, which support the stem growing in any direction, such as passion flower and grape vines.

Progression

Key Stage	Development of ideas
EYFS	· Pupils should explore and respond to different natural phenomena in their settings and on trips. · Pupils should be encouraged to talk about what they see, using a wide vocabulary. · Pupils begin to understand the need to respect and care for the natural environment and all living things. · Pupils should explore the natural world around them.
KS1 (ages 5-7)	· Pupils should be able to identify and name a variety of common wild and garden plants, including deciduous and evergreen trees. · Pupils should identify and describe the basic structure of a variety of common flowering plants, including trees. · Pupils should be able to observe and describe how seeds and bulbs grow into mature plants. · Pupils should find out and describe how plants need water, light and a suitable temperature to grow and stay healthy.
KS2 (ages 7-11)	· Pupils should be able to identify and describe the functions of different parts of flowering plants: roots, stem/trunk, leaves and flowers. · Pupils should explore the requirements of plants for life and growth (air, light, water, nutrients from soil, and room to grow) and how they vary from plant to plant. · Pupils should investigate the way in which water is transported within plants.
KS3 (ages 11-14)	· Pupils should know that plants make carbohydrates in their leaves by photosynthesis and by gaining mineral nutrients and water from the soil via their roots.

Roots

The big idea of roots is that they provide anchorage for plants to prevent them from falling over. Roots also absorb water and nutrients from the soil and convey this nourishment to the rest of the plant through tissues in the stem. Tiny root hairs protrude from the root, which help with absorption.

To make the most of roots, teachers should show pupils a variety of plants with living roots. These can be grown in pots for easy access to the roots – gently shake off the compost. Roots can be examined with magnifying glasses or, even better, a microscope. Teachers should also show pupils a range of root vegetables such as carrots and parsnips. Seeds can be grown in plastic containers so that pupils can see the roots developing. Broad beans are particularly good for this activity as they germinate quickly and can survive without soil for a few weeks.

The key problem with roots is finding plants with strong root systems to show the pupils. It is very difficult to pull up a plant growing outside with the roots intact, so growing or buying plants in pots is preferable.

Roots growing from a germinating bean.

● Key questions

○ **What are the functions of the root?**
The functions of the root are to anchor the plant and to absorb water and nutrients.

○ **Can plants survive without roots?**
A plant without roots will struggle to absorb nutrients and water from the ground. Also, it will not be able to stay upright. Over time, some plants will grow new roots if all the other conditions are favourable.

○ **Do roots always grow downwards?**
Yes, plant roots will always grow downwards towards a water source. A good experiment to show this is to rotate a broad bean seed that has germinated so that the new root points upwards. Over time, the root will begin to bend downwards again.

○ **Will a seed grow roots if there is no soil?**
Yes, as long as it is provided with warmth and moisture.

○ **Can plants grow without soil?**
Yes, some plants can grow without soil as long as their roots are in water that is rich in minerals and nutrients (this is how hydroponic plants are grown).

Common misconceptions

○ **Plants eat food and this food comes from the soil via the roots.**
Plants need chemicals such as magnesium and nitrates from the soil to make proteins and chlorophyll, but these are classed as nutrients, not food. Plants make their own food, which is called glucose, through the process of photosynthesis, which occurs in the leaves.

○ **All plants have roots.**
Some plants called *Bryophytes*, such as moss and liverworts, have no roots, leaves or stems. They are flowerless plants that grow in clumps.

○ **You cannot eat roots.**
Some pupils will not believe that vegetables such as carrots and parsnips are roots. Teachers should show pupils a variety of root vegetables and explain that these grow under the ground.

○ **Roots only grow in the ground.**
The roots of most plants lie underground; however, in some plants, the roots are aerial (such as orchids), or in water (such as pond lilies).

○ **Plants only reproduce by producing seeds.**
Plants can also reproduce asexually through vegetative propagation; for example, you can grow a new carrot plant by cutting off the top of a carrot and putting it into the soil.

Progression

Key Stage	Development of ideas
EYFS	· Pupils should explore and respond to different natural phenomena in their settings and on trips. · Pupils should be encouraged to talk about what they see, using a wide vocabulary, and begin to understand the need to respect and care for the natural environment and all living things. · Pupils should have the opportunity to explore the natural world around them.
KS1 (ages 5-7)	· Pupils should be able to identify and name a variety of common wild and garden plants, including deciduous and evergreen trees. · Pupils should be able to identify and describe the basic structure of a variety of common flowering plants, including trees. · Pupils should observe and describe how seeds and bulbs grow into mature plants. · Pupils should find out and describe how plants need water, light and a suitable temperature to grow and stay healthy.
LKS2 (ages 7-9)	· Pupils should be able to identify and describe the functions of different parts of flowering plants: roots, stem/trunk, leaves and flowers. · Pupils should explore the requirements of plants for life and growth (air, light, water, nutrients from soil, and room to grow) and how they vary from plant to plant. · Pupils should investigate the way in which water is transported within plants.
UKS2 (ages 9-11)	· Pupils should find out about different types of reproduction, including sexual and asexual reproduction in plants (cuttings, tubers, bulbs) and sexual reproduction in animals.
KS3 (ages 11-14)	· Plants make carbohydrates in their leaves by photosynthesis and by gaining mineral nutrients and water from the soil via their roots.

What is soil?

The big idea is that soil is a thin layer of material that covers the Earth's surface and is formed by the weathering and natural erosion of rocks. Soil is a mixture of tiny particles of organic materials (plant- and animal-based) and inorganic materials (rocks and minerals) plus air and water. Different soils have different properties depending on their composition.

To make the most of this topic, provide pupils with a variety of different soil samples including peat, clay, sandy, chalky and loamy soil. You can look at the samples under a microscope at different magnifications to classify the soils depending on their colour and texture. You can test the water retention and porosity of soils by putting different samples of soils in funnels and timing how long it takes for water to pass through them.

The key problem with teaching this topic is obtaining the variety of different soil samples. While these can be purchased from educational resource providers, they will not contain larger pieces of organic material or invertebrates. It is therefore important to show pupils naturally-occurring soil as well as shop-bought samples. Another problem is hygiene. Soil contains many millions of bacteria and other microorganisms, most of which are harmless, but some are potentially dangerous. Insist on glove-wearing and good hand-washing during and after handling soil. Testing the soils with water can be quite messy, so consider doing these practical activities outside. Lastly, storing large quantities of soil samples can be problematic, so find a dry, suitable place in which to keep them.

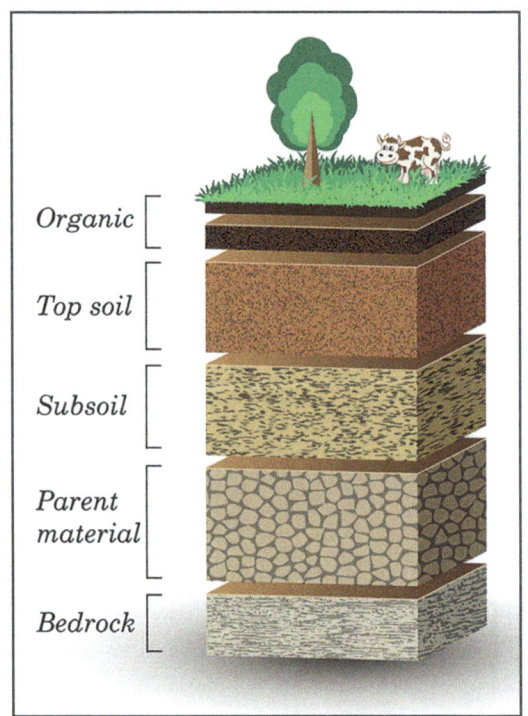

Organic

Top soil

Subsoil

Parent material

Bedrock

A cross-section of soil.

● Key questions

○ **Are all soils the same?**

○ **What can you see in the soil (living and non-living)?**

○ **What colour and texture is the soil?**

○ **What size are the particles in the soil?**

○ **Is the soil porous?**

○ **How much water does the soil let through?**

○ **Is there any plant or animal material present in the soil?**

○ **Would this be a good soil for roots to anchor a plant?**

● Common misconceptions

○ **Compost and soil are the same thing.**
Compost is made of decomposed organic material, while soil contains other substances including minerals and rock particles. Soil is a natural product that is formed in the environment, whereas compost is intentionally produced.

○ **All soil is brown.**
Soil is actually a range of colours and this depends on the rocks that it is made up of; for example, chalky soil will be whiter and sandy soil more yellow in colour.

○ **All soil is the same texture.**
Some soils may be rougher than others, or contain small rocks. Some soils may be smooth. The texture of the soil influences the amount of water that it can hold.

○ **Plants get food from the soil, or eat soil.**
Plants do not get food from the soil, they use the process of photosynthesis to create their own food. To grow successfully, plants absorb mineral nutrients, such as calcium and iron-nitrogen from the soil.

● Progression

Key Stage	Development of ideas
EYFS	· Pupils should know that the land is covered in soil and know that plants grow in the soil and that animals such as worms live in the soil. · Pupils should be encouraged to have interactions with the outdoors to foster curiosity and be given the freedom to touch, smell and hear the natural world around them during hands-on experiences.
KS1 (ages 5-7)	· Pupils should use the local environment throughout the year to learn about and answer questions about plants growing in their habitat. · Pupils should observe and describe how seeds and bulbs grow into mature plants. · Pupils should be introduced to the requirements of plants for germination, growth and survival.
KS2 (ages 7-11)	· Pupils should recognise that soils are made from rocks and organic matter. · Pupils should explore different kinds of rocks and soils, including those in the local environment. · Pupils should explore different soils and identify similarities and differences between them. · Pupils should investigate what happens when rocks are rubbed together, or what changes occur when they are in water. · Pupils should be be able to raise and answer questions about the way in which soils are formed. · Pupils should recognise that environments can change and that this can sometimes pose dangers to living things.
KS3 (ages 11-14)	· Pupils should understand the composition of the Earth. · Pupils should understand the structure of the Earth.

Habitats and ecosystems

The big idea of habitats and ecosystems is that, for organisms to live, there is an interdependence between them and that green plants are key in this.

To make the most of teaching habitats and ecosystems, it is important that pupils already have an awareness of their natural environment and that not all plants and animals are able to live in all environments. They should learn that plants and animals have features (adaptations) that enable them to best survive in a particular environment. There are living (biotic) and non-living (abiotic) elements to any environment. The habitat is a place where a plant or animal lives and the ecosystem is the interrelationship between the living things and their physical environment.

The key problem with habitats and ecosystems is that they are vast topics taught through examples that are distant to the pupils. It is good to be able to draw upon local examples as well as the global examples that are more commonly used.

Common habitats on Earth

● Key questions

○ **What do plants and animals get from this habitat that they need to survive?**
Using images to support this learning is key.

○ **What would happen to this habitat if the temperature increased?**

○ **What different roles do plants play in this ecosystem or environment?**

● Common misconceptions

○ **Plants and animals change to suit their environment.**
It is important that, from the start of this learning, pupils realise that plants and animals do not adapt there and then. They have adaptations that allow them to survive.

○ **Animals and plants choose where to live.**
Children may believe that plants and animals make a conscious choice where to live – this is not the case! Typically, plants and animals that are not well suited to their environment simply die.

○ **A habitat is a 'home'.**
Children should be made aware that the plants and animals live there, but should be discouraged from considering this as a 'home'.

● Progression

Key Stage	Development of ideas
EYFS	· Pupils should explore and talk about the places around them where things live. This might be a nature area, but could be any place that plants, bugs or other living things can be found, such as moss growing on a wall or weeds between paving stones.
KS1 (ages 5-7)	· Pupils should learn that most living things live in habitats to which they are suited. · Pupils should be able to describe how different habitats provide for the basic needs of different kinds of animals and plants, and how they depend on each other. · Pupils should identify and name a variety of plants and animals in their habitats, including micro-habitats.
KS2 (ages 7-11)	· Pupils should be able to recognise that environments can change and that this can pose danger to living things. · Pupils should identify and name a variety of living things in their local and wider environment.
KS3 (ages 11-14)	· Pupils should learn about interdependence of organisms in an ecosystem, including food webs and insect-pollinated crops. · Pupils should know how organisms affect, and are affected by, their environment, including the accumulation of toxic materials.

Natural selection

The big idea of natural selection is that it explains **how** one group of organisms (a species) evolves into another (there are other ways, but these are much rarer and not necessary for primary pupils to learn about). There is variety within groups of the same organisms. Some individuals have features or display behaviours (adaptations) that give them a better chance of surviving. These organisms have a higher probability of reproducing. Offspring are more likely to be similar to their parents and have these features that aid survival.

To make the most of helping pupils to understand this process, you should give them as many opportunities to recognise that there is variation within a group of the same organisms as possible. For example, if learning about male deer, you could study the size of antlers and how they differ across the group. Discussions could be had about the benefits and drawbacks of large and small antlers.

In addition to this, it is important to refer to an organism's features and behaviours and how they help it to survive in its habitat. Give pupils the chance to consider what might happen if the organism's habitat changed.

The key problem with understanding natural selection is that it is driven by chance. If a group of organisms do not have a necessary feature that aids survival, this cannot miraculously appear, or be wished up by an organism. It is down to luck whether any of the members of the group already possess it.

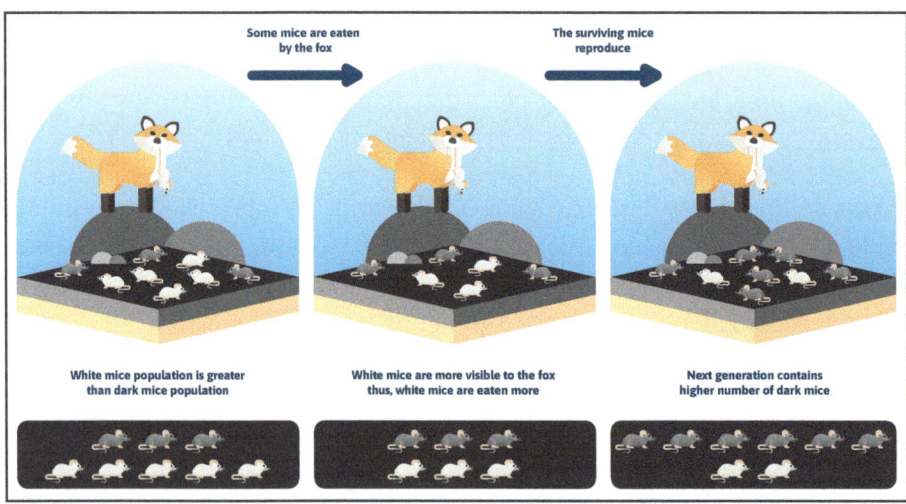

Key questions

○ **What differences can you see within this group of animals/plants?**
Appropriate answers include size of leaves, colour of fur, etc.

○ **How does this (named) feature/behaviour help this (named) organism survive in its habitat?**
Appropriate answer: linking the feature to the specified habitat.

O **What would happen if this (named) organism's habitat changed?**
Appropriate answers include acknowledging how certain features may develop over time depending on how the habitat changed.

O **What are the steps of natural selection?**
See explanation provided in the first paragraph.

O **Can you suggest how a (named) organism evolved its (named) feature?**
The steps of natural selection are described and applied to a specific organism. Sensible suggestions are made for how the named feature aided survival.

Common misconceptions

O **What is 'survival of the fittest'?**
Sometimes natural selection is referred to as 'survival of the fittest'. Children can often, incorrectly, confuse the term 'fit' with features related to speed and strength. 'Fit' organisms have features or exhibit behaviours that help them to survive and subsequently reproduce. For example, a stick insect that has better camouflage is said to be 'fit'.

O **Evolution on demand. Organisms cannot choose to evolve.**
Giraffes did not evolve longer necks from a group of horse-like animals (common ancestors to the giraffe) because they needed them for reaching food found higher up. It just so happened that, within the group, some had longer necks. These were more likely to survive because they could reach extra food and then could reproduce.

O **Evolution through underuse or overuse.**
Often, pupils think that the overuse or underuse of a feature can result in this being passed on to the organism's offspring. An example of this misunderstanding is that ostriches have short, stumpy wings because their parents did not use their wings very often.

Progression

Key Stage	Development of ideas
EYFS	· Pupils are asked to name and describe familiar plants and animals and observe where they are found.
KS1 (ages 5-7)	· Pupils learn about a range of habitats and the animals and plants that inhabit them. They learn about the simple features/behaviours that organisms possess that make them suited for living in a specific habitat. · Pupils will also learn about the life cycle of some animals and that the offspring will look similar but not identical to their parents. It is likely that there will be a greater focus on animals than on plants.
LKS2 (ages 7-9)	· Pupils are asked to recognise that environments can change and that this can sometimes pose dangers to living things. Although not explicit, this may introduce them to extinction.
UKS2 (ages 9-11)	· Pupils are asked to identify in more detail how animals and plants are adapted to suit their environment and that adaptation may lead to evolution. The term 'natural selection' is not used, but it is likely that it will be studied.
KS3 (ages 11-14)	· Pupils learn that the variety between individuals is due to the inheritance of genetic material and exposure to environmental factors. They study natural selection as the mechanism that drives evolution in more detail. They also learn about extinction.

The senses

The big idea about the senses is that they are our body's way of interacting with the world around us. Humans have five basic senses: sight, hearing, taste, smell and touch. Each sense is connected to specific organs that collect information, which is then processed by our brains, helping us to understand and respond to our environment.

To make the most of this idea, relate the senses to daily experiences. Conduct activities that allow pupils to understand each of their senses individually, such as taste tests or sound identification games. Discuss how we use different senses in different situations, and how they work together to give us a full picture of our surroundings.

The key challenge in teaching about the senses lies in the complexity of the underlying biological processes. Explaining how sensory organs collect information and how our brains interpret these signals can involve abstract concepts and unfamiliar vocabulary. Hands-on activities, models and diagrams can be particularly useful for visualising these processes and making the abstract more concrete.

● Key questions

O **Can you name some things that we can only know because we can see them?**

O **What happens when you close your eyes? Can you still see things?**

O **How does a sound change if it's far away, or close by?**

O **How can you tell if something is hot or cold?**

O **Can you describe how different textures feel, such as sandpaper, a smooth rock, or a fluffy pillow?**

O **Why is it important to be able to feel things?**

O **How does your tongue help you to enjoy your favourite food?**

O **What happens when you try to eat something while your nose is pinched? Does it taste the same?**

O **How can our noses warn us of danger (like smoke from a fire)?**

O **Can you tell what someone is cooking just by smelling?**

○ How do our senses help us to understand the world around us?

○ Can you think of a time when you used all your senses at once?

○ How do people manage when one of their senses doesn't work (for example, if they can't see or hear)?

Common misconceptions

○ **Humans only have five senses.**
While the basic five (sight, hearing, taste, smell and touch) are most commonly taught, some scientists argue that we have additional senses, such as balance, temperature, and proprioception (body awareness).

○ **All senses function independently.**
Pupils often don't realise that our senses work together to help us to understand our environment. For example, flavour is a combination of both taste and smell.

○ **The tongue has different regions for each taste.**
The idea that certain tastes can only be sensed in specific regions of the tongue is outdated. All taste sensations can come from all parts of the tongue.

○ **Eyes see everything like a camera.**
Many pupils believe that our eyes work like a camera, capturing a picture of the world. In reality, our brains play a significant role in interpreting the signals from our eyes to create our perception of the world.

Progression

Key Stage	Development of ideas
EYFS	· Pupils can begin by exploring different textures, smells, sounds, tastes and sights in their environment, forming a basic understanding of the five senses.
KS1 (ages 5-7)	· Pupils should learn about the human body, including the basic functions of the senses. · They can learn about how the senses help us to interact with the world.
LKS2 (ages 7-9)	· Pupils should delve deeper into the function of the senses, learning more about the specific organs involved and how they collect information.
UKS2 (ages 9-11)	· Pupils should be able to learn more detailed exploration of the senses, including how the brain processes sensory information.
KS3 (ages 11-14)	· Pupils should deepen their understanding of human biology, including the intricate processes involved in sensory perception. This can include a more detailed study of the nervous system and how it interprets sensory information.

Muscles

The big idea is that muscles bring about movement in the human body through contracting. They work closely with the skeleton by attaching to bones, which then create movement as they pull on them. In addition to these skeletal muscles, there are also smooth muscles that are found as part of organs such as in the digestive system. Cardiac muscle is found in the heart.

To make the most of this idea, you should focus pupils' attention on the physical movements that we can see as a result of muscle contractions before exploring those that are not visible. Links should be made with exercise, health and diet.

Muscular contractions are controlled by the nervous system. The muscle fibres are made up of protein – which is one of the reasons that this is an important part of the diet. Electrical impulses cause the movement of the fibres, which cause the muscle to get shorter and so the contraction takes place.

The key problem with learning about muscles is that the concept can be quite abstract and pupils will think about movement only in the broadest sense, but not link this with the movement of smaller muscles such as within the eye, or the 'unseen' movements within the digestive system and other organs.

Some of the muscles within the human body.

Frontalis	Temporalis
Orbicularis oculi	Nasalis
Sternocleidomastoid	Orbicularis oris
Deltoid	Rotator cuff
Pectoralis major	Biceps brachii
Rectus abdominis	Brachialis
Abdominal external oblique	Pronator teres
Iliopsoas	Brachioradialis
Quadriceps femoris	Adductor muscles
Peroneus longus	Tibialis anterior
Peroneus brevis	

Key questions

○ **Why do we need muscles?**
Muscles are needed for physical activities including movement, breathing and playing musical instruments! They are also key for other smaller movements, such as blinking. Muscles enable us to maintain stability through their work with the skeleton. They also play important roles in digestion and circulation and generate heat, which helps to maintain body temperature.

○ **Can we make muscles bigger?**
The size of muscle fibres can be increased through specific exercises and usually involves weight training or resistance training. There also needs to be adequate nutrition related to this and the diet of elite sports people will often be higher in protein as a result of the work that their muscles do and the strength or endurance required.

○ **How many muscles do we have in the human body?**
There are over 600 muscles in the human body. The smallest of the muscles is found in the ear and is just over 1 mm in length. The most active muscles are those in your eyes, used for looking in all directions as well as blinking. The thigh muscle is one of the largest muscles that we have.

● Common misconceptions

○ **Contraction and relaxation bring about moving.**
Many muscles work in pairs. One set contracts to bring about a movement – such as pointing your toes upwards – and then another set contracts to move them back down. It is not the relaxing of the first set of muscles that causes the movement.

○ **Muscle turns into fat.**
Muscle and fat are two separate types of tissue, and one cannot turn into the other. However, it is possible to lose muscle and gain fat, or vice versa, through changes in diet and exercise habits.

○ **Muscles are only on arms and legs.**
As these are the most obvious to pupils, they often think that muscles in the human body are only those most visible through movement.

● Progression

Key Stage	Development of ideas
EYFS	· Pupils are encouraged to develop large and small muscle coordination. · Pupils should be provided with regular access to floor space indoors for movement. · Pupils should be encouraged to use precision and accuracy when beginning and ending movements.
KS1 (ages 5-7)	· Pupils should be able to describe the importance for humans of exercise, eating the right amounts of different types of food, and hygiene.
LKS2 (ages 7-9)	· Pupils should be able to identify that animals, including humans, need the right types and amount of nutrition, and that they cannot make their own food; they get nutrition from what they eat · Pupils should identify that humans and some other animals have skeletons and muscles for support, protection and movement.
UKS2 (ages 9-11)	· Pupils should recognise the impact of diet, exercise, drugs and lifestyle on the way that their bodies function.
KS3 (ages 11-14)	· Pupils should learn the structure and functions of the human skeleton, to include support, protection, movement and making blood cells. · Pupils should learn the interaction between skeleton and muscles, including the measurement of force exerted by different muscles. · Pupils should know the function of muscles and examples of antagonistic muscles.

Respiration

The big idea is that all organisms require food to live. During respiration, the food that we eat reacts with oxygen, producing carbon dioxide and water and this enables the organism to carry out its life processes. To make the most of this idea, you should focus pupils' attention on why they require food and provide them with a range of life processes to demonstrate this.

This should include examples from:

1. Animals, such as moving, keeping warm (in mammals and birds), growing, maintaining the body and reproducing (e.g. making eggs); and

2. Plants, such as growing, and making seeds.

You can use muscles as an example to help pupils to make links between the effect of exercise on breathing and heart rate and relate this to the muscle's extra demand for food and oxygen to be able to contract more.

The key problem with respiration is that it is an abstract concept that occurs in individual cells. At Key Stage 2 (ages 7-11), pupils are likely to only have been introduced to organs. Cells (which organs are made from) and respiration are not explicitly taught until Key Stage 3 (ages 11-14), but are unifying concepts for processes such as breathing, blood circulation and feeding.

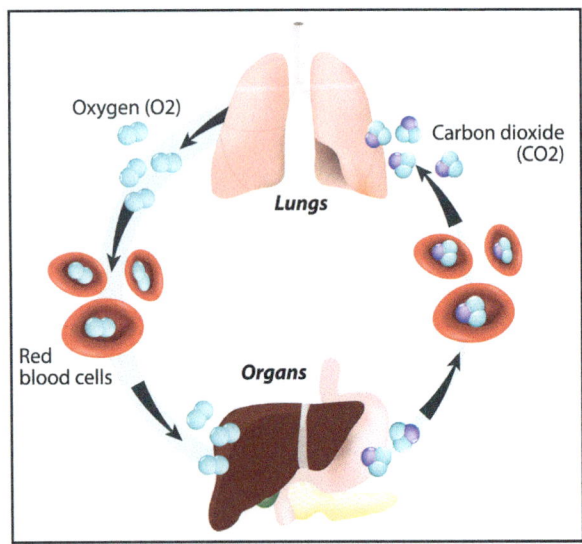

Respiration in cells.

Key questions

○ **Why does your body require food for respiration?**
Your body requires food for everyday activities and longer term processes such as moving, growing, keeping at the correct temperature and reproducing.

○ **Why do the cells in your muscles need to respire?**
So that they can contract and bring about movement.

○ **How does the muscle get what it requires for contracting?**
The muscles require food and oxygen, which it gets from the blood. The process of respiration is the reaction between these.

○ **Why does your breathing rate increase when you exercise?**
More oxygen is required by your muscles. You breathe faster so that more oxygen is moved into the lungs and can be transported in your blood. You also breathe faster because more carbon dioxide is made by your muscles. This is removed from the blood into the lungs and breathed out.

○ **Why does your heart rate increase when you exercise?**
Food and oxygen are carried in the blood to your muscles. When you exercise, your muscles require more oxygen and food so that the muscles can contract more.

Common misconceptions

○ **Respiration is often incorrectly used as a synonym for breathing.**
These two processes are not the same thing! Breathing is where we bring air into the lungs. Respiration is a chemical reaction that takes place in cells.

○ **Respiration only happens in the muscles.**
Probably because muscles are often used as an example of the site of respiration, pupils may think that this is the only place where it occurs. Respiration occurs in the cells of all organs.

○ **Plants don't respire.**
Plants photosynthesise and respire. All living things respire.

Progression

Key Stage	Development of ideas
EYFS	· Pupils should have the opportunity to observe and handle a range of plants and animals and learn about some of their life cycles.
KS1 (ages 5-7)	· Pupils learn about the different types of human and plant organs. At this stage, they may only identify human organs such as the head, arms and legs, but they may be taught about the heart and lungs. They also understand that animals are alive because they breathe, move and reproduce.
LKS2 (ages 7-9)	· Pupils learn about the skeletal and muscular system.
UKS2 (ages 9-11)	· Pupils are asked to identify and name the main parts of the human circulatory system, and describe the functions of the heart, blood vessels and blood. They should be able to describe how nutrients and water are transported around the human body.
KS3 (ages 11-14)	· Pupils should learn about cells and aerobic respiration (respiration that requires oxygen and has been described here).

Digestion

The big idea is that digestion is the process that breaks down food into smaller molecules, which the body can use.

To make the most of this idea, you should focus pupils' attention on the physical movement of the food through the digestive system, the use of chemicals to aid the breakdown (acid in the stomach and enzymes in the different parts of the system) and links with respiration making use of broken-down sugars (into glucose).

Children generally engage well with this topic because it ends with poo! They can make tangible links with the physical aspects of chewing food to start the digestion process and recognise that changes happen throughout the process. It is important to model the use of scientific vocabulary – using oesophagus, for example, not 'food tube'.

The key problem with learning about digestion is that there are a number of parts of the system to learn about, each with different functions. There are models that can be used – such as banana, orange juice and cereal being pushed through muslin or tights – which are limited in their accuracy. Whilst engaging for the pupils, it is important that we highlight the continuous nature of the digestive system from mouth to anus.

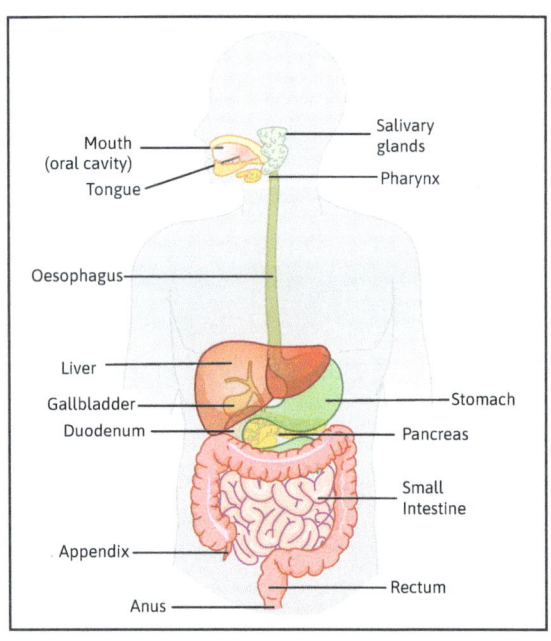

The digestive system.

● Key questions

○ **Why is digestion needed?**
Our food contains the nutrients that we need, but not in a form we can easily use. The process of digestion breaks down large insoluble molecules into smaller soluble ones, which can be absorbed into the blood for transport around the body to where they are used.

How is food broken down during digestion?

Mechanical digestion happens as we chew food in our mouths and the physical churning in our stomachs also breaks the food down. Food is mixed with saliva in the mouth, which softens the food for swallowing. The stomach acid acts to kill bacteria and create the best pH for some of the enzymes to start working. The acid is neutralised by bile (which enters from the gall bladder), as the 'food', now known as chyme, moves into the small intestine. Further enzymes break down the food in the small intestine and water is removed as it moves through the large intestine. The useful parts are reabsorbed through the walls of the intestine before the waste is excreted.

Common misconceptions

The oesophagus and trachea are the same.

Children often think that there is one tube that goes from the back of the throat into the body. The oesophagus is the one that we use when we swallow food to be moved to the stomach, and the trachea goes to the lungs. Children can be asked about when they have a drink that 'goes down the wrong way' and the impact that this has.

The parts of digestive system are separate.

Whilst there are different parts to the digestive system, these are in effect one continuous tube that has differentiated organs with specific functions. This is where models can be problematic, so choosing them carefully is important.

Only humans have a digestive system.

Mammals have a very similar structure and function to their digestive systems, and it should be considered a mammalian, rather than human, representation.

Progression

Key Stage	Development of ideas
EYFS	· Pupils should be able to make healthy choices about food.
KS1 (ages 5-7)	· Pupils should be able to identify, name, draw and label the basic parts of the human body and say which part of the body is associated with each sense. · Pupils should find out about and describe the basic needs of animals, including humans, for survival (water, food and air).
LKS2 (ages 7-9)	· Pupils should be able to identify that animals, including humans, need the right types and amount of nutrition, and that they cannot make their own food; they get nutrition from what they eat. · Pupils should be able to describe the simple functions of the basic parts of the digestive system in humans.
UKS2 (ages 9-11)	· Pupils should be able to describe the ways in which nutrients and water are transported within animals, including humans.
KS3 (ages 11-14)	· Pupils should learn about the tissues and organs of the human digestive system, including adaptations to function and how the digestive system digests food (enzymes simply as biological catalysts).

Blood circulation

The big idea is that blood moves around the body in vessels, pumped by the heart. The blood carries with it essential nutrients, oxygen and waste products such as carbon dioxide.

To make the most of this idea, you should focus pupils' attention on the structures that support circulation as well as the pathway that the blood takes.

This is an area with which pupils are often familiar, due to their own and others' injuries, but also one that causes some confusion.

The key problem with blood circulation is that there are a number of different vessels, complicated by a double circulation system and that, when we refer to left- and right-hand sides, this is not how we are looking at a diagram but rather how it is positioned within the body.

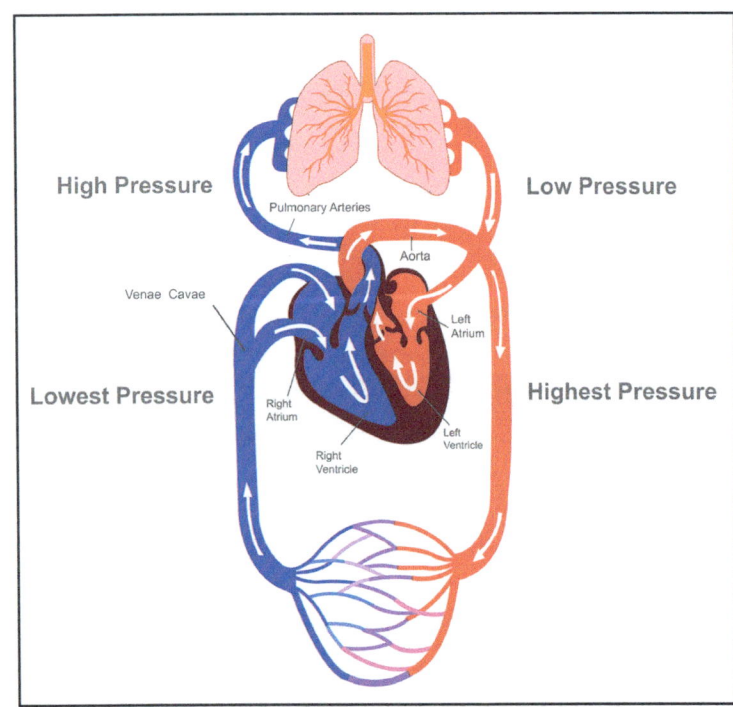

The mammalian circulatory system.

Key questions

O **What does our blood actually do?**
Our blood has a number of different roles. Simply, it transports essential things around our bodies and removes ones we need to get rid of. It also has a key role in keeping us healthy through our immune system.

O **Do all animals have blood?**
No, but most do! Some worms and cnidarians (jellyfish, coral and anemones) do not, but a lot of animals have some form of fluid that does a similar job to blood, to carry oxygen to tissues and remove carbon dioxide.

Common misconceptions

O **Blood is blue.**
In part due to the diagrams commonly used, which show deoxygenated blood as blue, and the colour of the veins under the skin, pupils often believe that blood is blue rather than red.

O **Blood is a pure substance.**
As blood components are not visible to the naked eye, pupils do not always realise that there are white and red blood cells, plasma and platelets that make it up.

O **Blood isn't contained within vessels.**
As blood is most often seen through cuts and injuries, the blood vessels are not visible so it looks as though the blood is just sitting under the skin rather than moved around through arteries, veins and capillaries.

Progression

Key Stage	Development of ideas
EYFS	· Pupils should be able to explore the natural world around them.
KS1 (ages 5-7)	· Pupils should have plenty of opportunities to learn the names of the main body parts (including head, neck, arms, elbows, legs, knees, face, ears, eyes, hair, mouth, teeth). · Pupils should find out about and describe the basic needs of animals, including humans, for survival (water, food and air). · Pupils should be able to describe the importance for humans of exercise, eating the right amounts of different types of food, and hygiene.
KS2 (ages 7-11)	· Pupils should be able to identify and name the main parts of the human circulatory system, and describe the functions of the heart, blood vessels and blood.
KS3 (ages 11-14)	· Pupils should learn about the structure and functions of the human skeleton, to include support, protection, movement and making blood cells. · Pupils should learn about the interaction between skeleton and muscles, including the measurement of force exerted by different muscles.

Solids, liquids and gases

The big idea of 'solids, liquids and gases' is that substances can be usefully categorised into these three states depending on their properties.

To make the most of this idea, pupils need to experience the properties of solids, liquids and gases and how they are defined. The three states of matter are solid, liquid and gas. A solid keeps its shape and has a fixed volume. A liquid has a fixed volume but changes in shape to fit the container. A liquid can be poured, forms pools and keeps a level, horizontal surface. A gas fills all available space; it has no fixed shape or volume.

The key problem with real objects and materials is that they don't always fit easily into the categories. Granular and powdery solids such as sugar and sand can be confused with liquids because they can be poured but, when poured, they form a heap and they do not keep a level surface when tipped. Each individual grain demonstrates the properties of a solid. In addition, it can be difficult for pupils to understand the concept of gas as it often can't be seen (including steam – we can only see the tiny condensed liquid water drops).

Solid – ice

Liquid – water

Gas – steam (we've used a thermal image (created using ChatGPT), because you can't see steam. The cloud you see leaving a kettle is condensed water droplets.)

● Key questions

○ **Is this material a solid, liquid or a gas?**
Ask for lots of different substances – starting with the obvious and then building up to more tricky substances such as flour, or sand. You may want to discuss tricky substances such as toothpaste.

○ **Can you pour this substance?**

○ **Does it hold its shape even if you put it into a different-shaped container?**

○ **Does this substance fill the container... and, if you take the lid off, does it fill the room?**

Common misconceptions

○ **Sand is a liquid because it can be poured.**
Granular and powdery solids like sand can be confused with liquids because they can be poured but, when poured, they form a heap and they do not keep a level surface when tipped. Each individual grain demonstrates the properties of a solid.

○ **You can see steam.**
Many people believe that you can see steam or water vapour (a gas), but steam and water vapour are transparent. What we commonly call 'steam' is actually the liquid water droplets made when steam cools and condenses.

Progression

Key Stage	Development of ideas
EYFS	· Pupils should understand some important processes and changes in the natural world around them, including the seasons and changing states of matter.
KS1 (ages 5-7)	· Pupils should be able to distinguish between an object and the material from which it is made. · Identify and name a variety of everyday materials, including wood, plastic, glass, metal, water and rock. · Pupils should be able to describe the simple physical properties of a variety of everyday materials. · Pupils should be able to compare and group together a variety of everyday materials on the basis of their simple physical properties · Pupils should be able to identify and compare the suitability of a variety of everyday materials, including wood, metal, plastic, glass, brick, rock, paper and cardboard for particular uses. · Pupils should find out how the shapes of solid objects made from some materials can be changed by squashing, bending, twisting and stretching.
KS2 (ages 7-11)	· Pupils should be able to compare and group materials together, according to whether they are solids, liquids or gases.
KS3 (ages 11-14)	· Pupils should learn about conservation of material and of mass, and reversibility, in melting, freezing, evaporation, sublimation, condensation, dissolving. · Pupils should be able to identify similarities and differences, including density differences, between solids, liquids and gases. · Pupils should learn about brownian motion in gases. · Diffusion in liquids and gases are driven by differences in concentration.

Changes of state

The big idea of 'changes of state' is that many materials can change between the three states of matter. The three states of matter that we look at in primary education are solid, liquid and gas.

To make the most of this topic, you should start with water as it is an easy way for pupils to see the changes of state and how they can be reversed. Link these changes to the water cycle. Using other substances such as chocolate, butter and wax can also show changes of state from solid to liquid and vice versa.

The key problem with changes of state is that it is hard to see substances other than water change state into gas form without specialist equipment, due to the temperatures needed.

Melt
→

←
Solidify

Evaporate
→

←
Condense

You can't see water vapour, it becomes visible only when it condenses back into tiny liquid water droplets

Ice cube – solid   **Water – liquid**   **Water vapour – gas**

● Key questions

○ **Is this a solid, liquid or a gas?**
Show many examples – start simple.

○ **Do all solids melt at the same temperature?**
No, all substances have different melting points.

○ **At what temperature does water change state?**
Water changes from ice to liquid water at 0 °C and from liquid water to steam at 100 °C (though this changes depending on the air pressure).

○ **How can I make my clothes dry faster?**
You can increase the rate of evaporation by increasing the temperature, or by moving air across the clothes (e.g. on a windy day).

○ **How does chocolate change when heated?**
It melts.

○ **How does fruit juice change when put in the freezer?**
It solidifies.

○ **How does a snowman change over time?**
It melts.

● Common misconceptions

○ **Melting is the same as dissolving.**
Dissolving needs a solvent to dissolve into (e.g. water). Melting requires heat. For example, you can dissolve salt in water easily, but to melt salt you need a temperature of 801 °C.

○ **Solids are hard and cannot break or change shape easily and are often in one piece.**
Solids (even some metals) can be soft and some can be easily shaped (e.g. butter or plasticine).

○ **You can see water vapour or steam.**
You can't see steam or water vapour – it is invisible. What we often call 'steam' is really condensation (tiny liquid water droplets).

○ **Clouds are made of water vapour or steam.**
They are made of tiny liquid water droplets.

● Progression

Key Stage	Development of ideas
EYFS	· Pupils should understand some important processes and changes in the natural world around them. Pupils should know the names of the states of water (ice, liquid water and steam).
KS1 (ages 5-7)	· Pupils should be able to distinguish between an object and the material from which it is made. · Pupils should be able to identify and name a variety of everyday materials, including wood, plastic, glass, metal, water, and rock. · Pupils should be able to describe the simple physical properties of a variety of everyday materials · Pupils should be able to compare and group together a variety of everyday materials on the basis of their simple physical properties. · Pupils should be able to identify and compare the suitability of a variety of everyday materials, including wood, metal, plastic, glass, brick, rock, paper and cardboard for particular uses. · Pupils should be able to find out how the shapes of solid objects made from some materials can be changed by squashing, bending, twisting and stretching.
LKS2 (ages 7-9)	· Pupils should compare and group materials together, as solids, liquids or gases. · Pupils should observe that some materials change state when they are heated or cooled, and measure or research the temperature at which this happens in degrees Celsius (°C). · Pupils should be able to identify the part played by evaporation and condensation in the water cycle and associate the rate of evaporation with temperature.
UKS2 (ages 9-11)	· Pupils should be able to use knowledge of solids, liquids and gases to decide how mixtures might be separated, including through filtering, sieving and evaporating. · Pupils should demonstrate that dissolving, mixing and changes of state are reversible changes. · Pupils should be able to explain that some changes result in the formation of new materials, and that this kind of change is not usually reversible, including changes associated with burning and the action of acid on bicarbonate of soda. · Pupils should compare and group materials together, as solids, liquids or gases. · Pupils should observe that some materials change state when they are heated or cooled, and measure or research the temperature at which this happens in degrees Celsius (°C). · Pupils should be able to identify the part played by evaporation and condensation in the water cycle and associate the rate of evaporation with temperature.
KS3 (ages 11-14)	· Pupils will learn about matter and physical changes including, conservation of material and of mass, and reversibility, in melting, freezing, evaporation, sublimation, condensation, dissolving. · Similarities and differences, including density differences, between solids, liquids and gases · Pupils will learn about Brownian motion in gases and about diffusion in liquids and gases driven by differences in concentration · Pupils should be able to know the difference between chemical and physical changes.

Separating mixtures

The big idea about separating mixtures is that a mixture is composed of different substances that are not chemically combined. Since the substances are not chemically bonded, they retain their original properties and can be separated using physical methods such as filtration, evaporation, distillation and chromatography.

To make the most of this idea, you should try to relate it to real-world examples and observations. For instance, discuss how sand can be separated from water using filtration, or how salt can be retrieved from saltwater using evaporation.

Demonstrating these methods through hands-on experiments can be particularly effective. It's important to highlight that the choice of method depends on the types of substances present in the mixture and their different physical properties.

The key problem in teaching the separation of mixtures is that it involves abstract concepts that aren't immediately visible. Understanding that a mixture is composed of different substances and the idea that these substances can be separated can be challenging. To overcome this, use tangible examples and visual aids such as diagrams and videos. Hands-on experiments are also very effective in helping pupils to visualise and understand the process of separation.

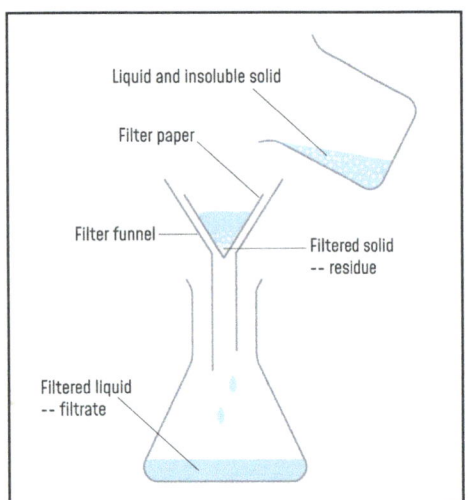
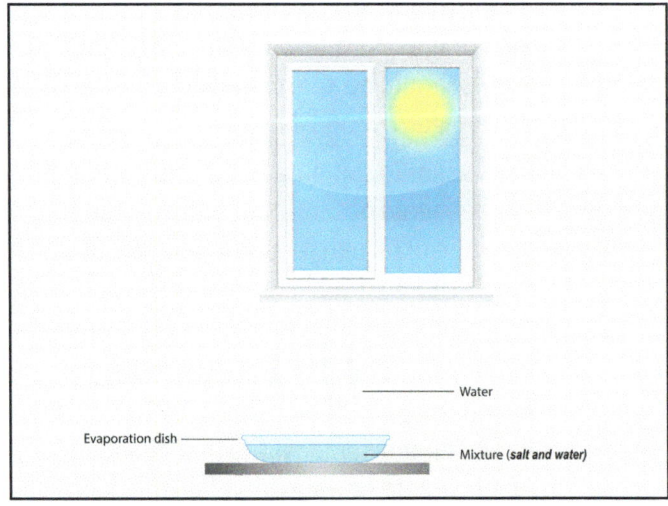

Separating salt and sand.

Key questions

○ **Can you think of a situation where we might need to separate a mixture?**
This question helps pupils to understand the practical implications of separating mixtures in real-life scenarios, such as cooking or cleaning water.

○ **What would you use to separate pebbles from sand?**
This question encourages pupils to think about the properties of different materials in a mixture and how these properties can help us to choose the right method to separate them.

○ **How could we get salt out of salty water?**
This question introduces the concept of evaporation as a method for separating mixtures.

○ **What happens to instant coffee in hot water and can we get the coffee granules back?**
This question encourages pupils to consider the concept of a soluble substance and how reversing the process might not always be straightforward.

● Common misconceptions

○ **Dissolved and evaporated substances no longer exist.**
Some pupils do not consider that these substances are still there, but in a different form.

○ **Only solids can be separated.**
Some pupils might think that only solid mixtures can be separated, while mixtures involving liquids or gases cannot. In reality, techniques such as distillation, evaporation and chromatography can be used to separate liquid mixtures, and gas mixtures can be separated using methods such as fractional distillation.

○ **All mixtures can be separated using the same method.**
There's often a belief that one method can be used to separate all types of mixtures. However, the method chosen for separation depends on the types of substances in the mixture and their properties.

○ **Evaporation and boiling are the same.**
Many pupils confuse evaporation with boiling. While both involve a change from a liquid to a gas state, evaporation occurs at any temperature, mainly at the surface of the liquid, whereas boiling occurs at a specific temperature throughout the entire liquid.

● Progression

Key Stage	Development of ideas
EYFS	· While there is no explicit mention of separating mixtures, pupils can start learning about it through activities such as separating items based on their characteristics, e.g. colour and size.
KS1 (ages 5-7)	· Pupils start to learn about the properties of materials, which can be used as a stepping stone to discuss how different materials or substances can be separated based on these properties.
LKS2 (ages 7-9)	· Pupils should observe that some materials change state when they are heated or cooled. They can use this knowledge to understand how mixtures might be separated, for instance, by heating a saltwater mixture to leave behind salt.
UKS2 (ages 9-11)	· Pupils should know that some materials will dissolve in liquid to form a solution, and describe how to recover a substance from a solution. They should use knowledge of solids, liquids and gases to decide how mixtures might be separated, including through filtering, sieving and evaporating.
KS3 (ages 11-14)	· Pupils should build on their knowledge of the properties of materials to experience how different separation techniques work. They should understand that different techniques are needed depending on the type of mixture, and be able to describe processes such as filtration, crystallisation, distillation and chromatography.

The properties of materials

The big idea of 'the properties of materials' is that when we can describe different substances accurately, we can find good uses for them.

To make the most of this idea, pupils need to experience many different materials and learn about their properties.

The key problem with learning about the properties of materials is applying the properties effectively to solve problems.

Testing three materials to see how waterproof they are.

Paper 'tent'   Cotton 'tent'   Polythene 'tent'

● Key questions

Property	Question	Possible answers
Waterproof	· What happens when you spray water on it? · What could you use this material for?	· The water runs off it. · A raincoat, a hat, a boat, waterproof socks…
Absorbent	· What happens to this material when it gets wet? · What could you use this material for?	· The water soaks into it. The material gets wet. · Towels, cloths for wiping up a wet mess, hankies, nappies, sanitary products…
Transparent	· Can you see through this material? · What could you use this material for?	· Yes · Windows, see-through packaging, glasses, phone screens…
Opaque	· Can you see through this material? · What could you use this material for?	· No · Curtains, clothes, envelopes…
Hard	· Can you change its shape or scratch this material easily? · What could you use this material for?	· No · Phone/watch screens (if transparent), cases, containers…
Soft	· Can you change this material's shape easily? · What could you use this material for?	· Yes · Pillows, cushions, clothes, bouncy castles…
Stiff	· What happens if you try to bend this material? · What could you use this material for?	· It would be hard to bend it. · A ruler, frames for glasses, building materials…

Property	Question	Possible answers
Flexible	· What happens if you try to bend this material? · What could you use this material for?	· It will bend easily. · Clothes, bags...
Brittle	· What happens if you try to bend this material? · What would happen if you made a bridge/ruler/cup out of this material?	· It might snap or shatter. · It might snap or shatter.
Insulating	· What happens if you put the material around something hot or cold? · What could you use this material for?	· The heat cannot travel through it easily. · Oven gloves, gloves, coats, flasks, blankets...

● Common misconceptions

○ **Everything solid is hard.**
One common misconception is that all solids are hard. In reality, solids can be soft, too, such as rubber, plasticine, or sponge.

○ **Only fabrics are materials.**
Materials are any substance, including liquids and gases, which can be used as part of a product. For example, water, air and steel are all examples of materials.

○ **The word 'rock' describes an object rather than a material.**
A rock is a chunk of rock, but rock can also be used to describe the substance, e.g. 'what type of rock is that table made from?'

● Progression

Key Stage	Development of ideas
EYFS	· While there is no explicit mention of materials and their uses, pupils are encouraged to experience a wide range of media and materials. They should have opportunities to share their thoughts, ideas and feelings through a variety of activities.
KS1 (ages 5-7)	· Pupils should be taught to distinguish between an object and the material from which it is made, identify and name a variety of everyday materials, and describe the simple physical properties of a variety of everyday materials. They should also be taught to compare and group together a variety of everyday materials on the basis of their simple physical properties, and find out how the shapes of solid objects made from some materials can be changed by squashing, bending, twisting and stretching. They should be taught some terms for describing materials accurately.
LKS2 (ages 7-9)	· Pupils should compare and group materials together based on their properties and use these properties to make choices about materials to solve problems. They should be able to describe the properties of materials accurately.
UKS2 (ages 9-11)	· Pupils should compare and group together everyday materials on the basis of their properties, including their hardness, solubility, transparency, conductivity (electrical and thermal) and response to magnets. They should also know that some materials will dissolve in liquid to form a solution, and describe how to recover a substance from a solution.
KS3 (ages 11-14)	· Pupils should build on their knowledge of atoms, elements and compounds. They should experience the properties of a broad range of materials. They should experience changes of state, in terms of the particle model. They should understand that materials can be arranged in a periodic table. They should learn how the properties of materials are related to their structures, and how they can be changed by chemical reactions.

Metals

The big idea of metals is that they have a number of properties that make them very useful materials. These include:

- that many are hard solids (although some aren't);
- that you can shape metals by bending or melting and pouring into a mould;
- that all metals conduct electricity (some better than others); and
- that **some** metals are magnetic: iron, steel, nickel and cobalt, but all of the others are **not** (you don't need to teach about nickel or cobalt).

To make the most of metals, pupils need to be able to identify several common examples, including iron, steel, copper, aluminium and brass. Pupils may also be familiar with gold and silver through jewellery. You can purchase a set of common metals (labelled) for use in class.

The key problem with metals is that there are so many of them and they all have different properties (this is also what makes them so useful).

Examples of different metals.

● Key questions

○ **How do you think this metal got its shape?**
Answers may include: it was melted and poured into a mould; it was bent, hammered or pressed; it was cut.

○ **Is this metal magnetic?**
Only if it is iron, steel (or nickel or cobalt).

○ **Does this metal conduct electricity?**
Yes, all metals conduct electricity, some better than others (copper is a very good conductor).

○ **What could you use this metal for?**
Aluminium is strong and light, so it's good for aircraft and patio doors; iron and steel are very strong, so good for bridges. Steel and aluminium can be recycled, which is more energy-efficient than obtaining new metal from ores.

○ **Where does metal come from?**
We get most metals from ores (rocks containing the metal). Some metals are pure elements (e.g. aluminium, iron, copper, gold), while others are mixtures (e.g. brass and steel. These are called alloys).

Common misconceptions

○ **All metals are hard.**
You won't have access to very soft metals, though some are only as hard as butter from the fridge and can be cut with a table knife.

○ **All metals are magnetic.**
Only iron, steel, nickel and cobalt are magnetic.

○ **Metals all have a high melting point.**
Some metals have a high melting point, but others, such as lead, are reasonably easy to melt. Mercury is a metal that is liquid at room temperature.

Progression

Key Stage	Development of ideas
KS1 (ages 5-7)	· It is useful for pupils to be able to separate metals from non-metals by simple properties (e.g. it is shiny, it is hard). Pupils should know the names of some common metals, such as gold, copper, iron and steel.
KS2 (ages 7-11)	· Pupils should be able to identify several different metals from their properties, such as silver, gold, copper, iron, steel and aluminium. · Pupils should know that some metals are attracted to magnets and that all metals conduct electricity. Pupils should know that most metals are solid at room temperature, but that they can be melted. · Pupils should know that some metals will oxidise if left outside (e.g. iron will rust and copper turns green/blue).
KS3 (ages 11-14)	· Pupils will be taught about changes of state in terms of the particle model. · Pupils will learn that some substances are pure elements (e.g. iron, gold, aluminium), while others are mixtures (e.g. steel and brass). · Pupils will learn some chemical reactions involving metals, including oxidation and reduction. They will learn about the reactivity of metals.

Reversible & irreversible changes

The big idea of reversible and irreversible changes is that some changes to materials (e.g. melting ice) are simple to reverse (pop the melted ice into a freezer), whereas other changes are difficult or impossible to reverse (e.g. you can't unburn toast).

To make the most of this idea, pupils need to be very familiar with several changes (and whether you can get back to the original conditions) in order for the categorisation to be meaningful. For example:

- melting and then solidifying (reversible);
- burning (irreversible);
- dissolving a substance and then evaporating the liquid to get the substance back (reversible); and
- cooking an egg (irreversible).

The key problem with reversible and irreversible change is that most changes are complicated. The simplest examples might be obvious (e.g. melting an ice cube, putting it back into the ice cube tray and freezing it), but, if the change involves changes in appearance when the process is reversed (e.g melted and re-solidified chocolate), or changes that are difficult or impossible to see (e.g evaporation), pupils will struggle to classify the change correctly.

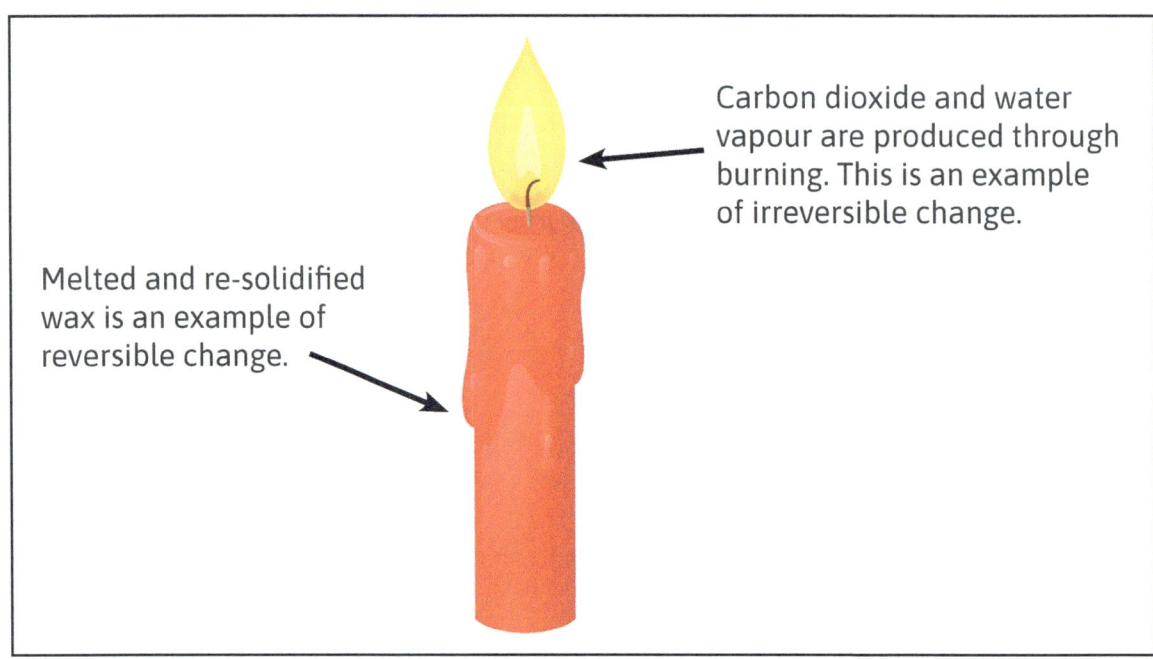

Carbon dioxide and water vapour are produced through burning. This is an example of irreversible change.

Melted and re-solidified wax is an example of reversible change.

Examples of reversible and irreversible changes.

Key questions

○ **What substance did you start with?**

○ **What change happened?**

○ **Can you change it back into the original substance? If so, how?**

Common misconceptions

○ **When a substance evaporates or dissolves, it has simply disappeared and can't come back.**
This will hinder pupils' understanding of reversible change.

○ **When a candle burns, it is the wick that produces the flame.**
In fact, it is the vaporised wax that is burning. The wick is there to carry the melted wax up into the flame.

○ **Substances disappear in combustion.**
In fact, many of the products of combustion are not visible (water vapour and carbon dioxide).

Progression

Key Stage	Development of ideas
EYFS & KS1 (ages 5-7)	· EYFS and KS1 is when learners begin to build up a bank of experiences about changes that can happen to materials. They will learn about melting and solidifying (ice and chocolate); they may learn about burning (candles).
KS2 (ages 7-11)	· Pupils will gain more experience of reversible changes when they learn about changes of state and dissolving. · Pupils need to categorise some common examples of reversible and irreversible changes. They may struggle due to a lack of experiences of irreversible changes, such as burning and corrosion.
KS3 (ages 11-14)	· Pupils learn about chemical changes as they learn about chemical reactions. · Pupils will understand reversible changes at a deeper level when they study the particle model.

Forces

The big idea is that forces can change how an object is moving and they can change an object's shape.

To make the most of teaching forces, pupils need to experience forces physically – causing forces with their muscles and experiencing forces acting on their bodies. They need to be taught how to describe the sensations in their bodies and the effects on their bodies, initially in simple language, but developing to use more scientific terminology.

The key problem with forces is that it is difficult to put the sensations that pupils have into words. You can support this with modelling and questioning. Gestures can help.

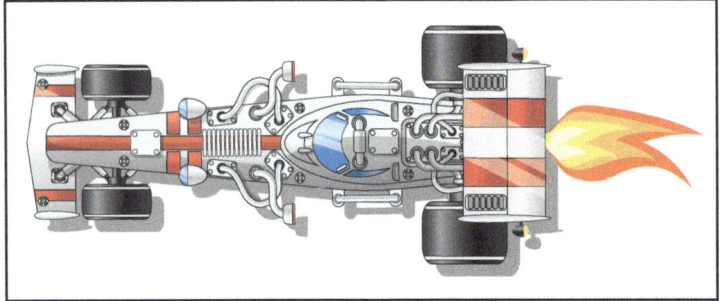

Forces can cause objects to speed up

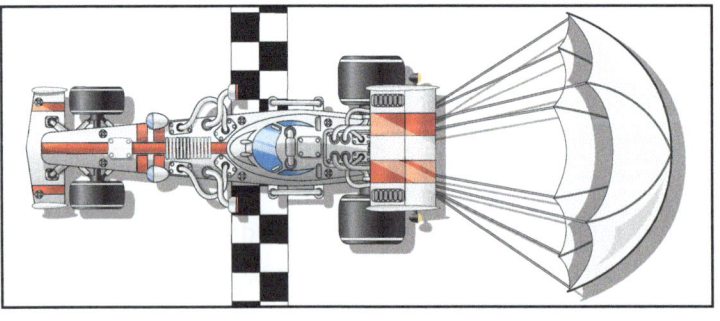

Forces can cause objects to slow down

Forces can cause objects to change direction

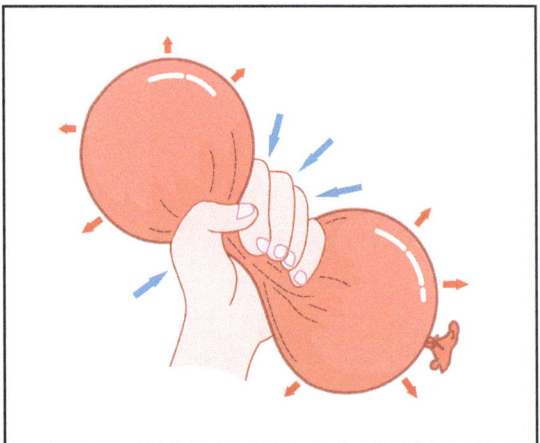

Forces can cause objects to change shape

Examples of forces changing speed, direction and shape.

● Key questions

○ What do you feel when a car/bus/train speeds up or slows down?

○ What do you feel when a car/bus/train goes around a corner?

○ What happens to the truck when you push it harder?

○ How can you slow the truck down?

○ What does it feel like when you jump off something, or go down a slide?

○ How can you bend that stick? What does it feel like when it snaps?

● Common misconceptions

○ **Forces can only be exerted by living things and some machines, but not by inanimate objects such as tables or shelves.**
Unmoving objects also exert forces, e.g. tables push upwards on an object, balancing the gravity pulling the object downwards.

○ **A force is needed to keep an object moving at a constant speed.**
An object will continue at a steady speed if there are no forces acting. It takes a force to make it speed up or slow down.

○ **Many pupils do not realise that you need at least two objects to have a force – something pushing and something pushed.**
You can never have one without the other.

● Progression

Key Stage	Development of ideas
EYFS	· Pupils should be encouraged to talk about the forces that they feel and the effects that they have.
KS1 (ages 5-7)	· Pupils should know that forces can cause objects to bend, stretch or squash and that forces can speed up an object or slow it down.
KS2 (ages 7-11)	· Pupils should know that forces need contact between two objects, but some forces can act at a distance (magnets, gravity and the force between charged objects). · Pupils should know that moving objects (such as balls and toy cars) slow down more quickly on some surfaces than others (friction). · Pupils should know that if you drop an object, it will fall towards the Earth because of the force of gravity acting between the Earth and the falling object. · Pupils should learn that objects such as tables and shelves can provide forces; for example, a table pushes up on an object, balancing the force of gravity pushing downwards. · Pupils should know that the solar system is held together by gravity (otherwise the planets would shoot off away from the Sun). · Pupils should know that air resistance, water resistance and friction act between moving surfaces. · Pupils should know that some mechanisms, including levers, pulleys and gears, allow a smaller force to have a greater effect.
KS3 (ages 11-14)	· Pupils should be able to use force arrows in diagrams. · Pupils should understand balanced and unbalanced forces. Pupils should know that forces deform objects, including springs. · Pupils should know that forces are measured in newtons.

Motion

The three big ideas of motion are:

- that objects can travel at a steady speed (scientists consider not moving to be a steady speed);
- that objects can speed up or slow down (accelerate and decelerate); or
- that objects can change direction.

To make the most of this idea, pupils should experience these three situations using many different examples. Don't forget that we consider not moving (stationary) as a steady speed.

The key problem with motion is being able to describe it accurately.

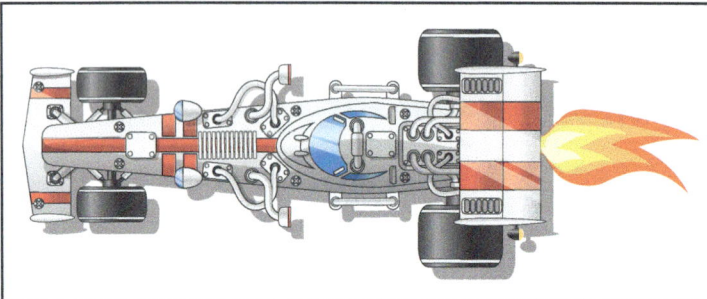

Speeding up

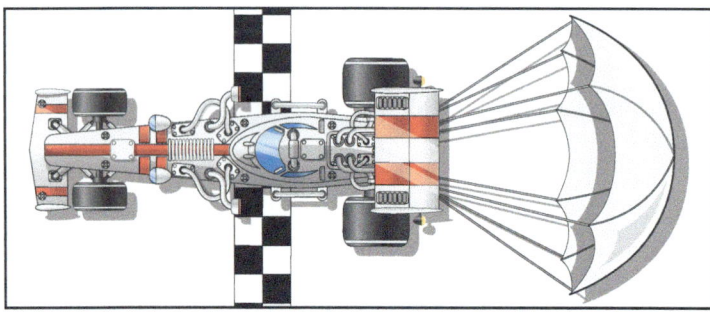

Slowing down

Changing direction

● Key questions

○ **Can you describe how this object is moving?**

- is it speeding up,
- slowing down, or
- changing direction?

● Common misconceptions

○ **Objects always slow down unless something is pushing them.**
Actually, an object always travels at a steady speed in a straight line, unless a force acts on it to change the speed or direction.

○ **When we accelerate (e.g. in a car) we feel as though we are pushed backwards.**
However, we are really being pushed forwards by the seat to speed us up.

● Progression

Key Stage	Development of ideas
EYFS & KS1 (ages 5-7)	· Pupils should have experience of and be able to describe how things move, including steady speed, speeding up and slowing down, and changing direction.
KS2 (ages 7-11)	· Pupils should be able to compare how things move on different surfaces and be introduced to the words 'accelerate' and 'decelerate'. · Pupils should be able to use ratios to explain why objects moving at steady speeds travel twice as far when they have been travelling for twice as long. · Pupils should know how to represent motion using arrows.
KS3 (ages 11-14)	· Pupils learn about speed and the quantitative relationship between average speed, distance and time (speed = distance / time). · Pupils should be able to represent a journey on a distance-time graph. · Pupils should understand relative motion: trains and cars passing one another.

Forces acting at a distance

The big idea of forces acting at a distance is that not all objects need to be touching to exert a force on each other.

To make the most of this idea, pupils should learn about three types of forces that act at a distance: **magnetism, electrostatic force** and **gravity**. There are many similarities between these forces and some differences:

Magnetism	Electrostatic Force	Gravity
Magnets can attract and repel.	Charges can attract and repel.	Gravity can only attract.
Each magnet has two poles: a north and a south. They cannot exist separately.	There are two types of charge: positive and negative. They can exist separately.	There is only one type of mass, measured in kilogrammes.
The force gets weaker as the distance between magnets increases.	The force gets weaker as the distance between charges increases.	The force gets weaker as the distance between objects increases.

The arrows in the diagrams show the **size** of the forces and the **direction**.

Key questions

○ **How are these three forces similar/different?**
- They are similar, because they act without touching and the forces get weaker the further apart the objects are.
- They are different, because charges are positive and negative and magnets have a north and south pole, whereas masses can only be positive.

○ **How can you tell that there is a force?**
There is a force because you can see an object's motion change. For example, a charged balloon will make a person's hair move.

Common misconceptions

○ **Many pupils believe that there is no gravity in space.**
There is gravity, otherwise planets would fly away from the Sun and moons from their planets. We couldn't have orbits without gravity.

○ **Many pupils see falling as 'natural' and not requiring an explanation.**
However, gravity can be explained as the force of attraction between two masses (such as the Earth and an apple).

○ **Many pupils think that all metals are magnetic.**
Only iron, steel, cobalt and nickel are magnetic. The others are not attracted to magnets.

Progression

Key Stage	Development of ideas
EYFS & KS1 (ages 5-7)	· Pupils should experience magnets attracting and repelling and be able to describe the forces that they feel. They should experience charged balloons to see them attract hair, small pieces of paper and walls. · Pupils may learn that the Moon and other planets in space also have gravity, but this might be stronger or weaker than on Earth (this could be taught through small world play). · Pupils should know that gravity pulls to the centre of the Earth (which is why people in Australia don't fall off). · Pupils should learn that there are different types of metal, and their names.
LKS2 (ages 7-9)	· Pupils should experience **attraction** and **repulsion** with magnets. They can test magnetic materials. · Pupils should learn that gravity holds planets in their orbits. They may learn the story of Newton sitting under the apple tree and realising that the gravity that pulls the apple to the ground is the same force that holds the Earth to the Sun and the Moon to the Earth.
UKS2 (ages 9-11)	· Pupils should understand that orbits happen because of gravity. · The force of attraction or repulsion gets weaker in non-contact forces the further apart the objects are. · Pupils should be able to compare and contrast magnetic force, electrostatic force and gravitational force.
KS3 (ages 11-14)	· Pupils will learn about magnetic, gravitational and electric fields. They will calculate the weight of objects using the gravitational field strength.

Light

The big idea about light is that it's a type of wave that enables us to see the world around us. Light travels from a source, reflects off objects and enters our eyes, which allows us to perceive those objects. It travels in straight lines and at an incredibly high speed.

To make the most of this idea, use daily experiences and simple experiments to explain the properties of light. For example, you could experience how we see objects differently in dim and bright light, or experiment with mirrors to demonstrate reflection.

The key challenge in teaching light is that you can't usually see the light travel from the source to the object – only the start and end points. Additionally, concepts such as reflection and refraction involve abstract ideas and scientific vocabulary. Using hands-on experiments, models and demonstrations can be beneficial in making these ideas more concrete.

Light emitted from a source, reflecting from a cat to the person's eye.

Key questions

What do we need to see things around us? Why is it hard to see in the dark?
We need a light source to shine onto the object. When the reflected light goes into our eyes, we can see it.

Can you name different sources of light?
Examples include: the Sun, the stars, lamps and torches. The Moon is not a source of light, because it does not produce light.

What happens when we switch on a lamp in a dark room? Why does this happen?
Light leaves the lamp and shines onto everything in the room. The light reflects off the objects. Some goes into our eyes and we can see the objects.

Can you think of some objects that let light pass through them and some objects that do not?
You can introduce transparent, translucent and opaque materials.

What happens when light hits a mirror? Can you explain why we can see our reflection in a mirror?
Light from a light source reflects off our bodies. Some of that light hits the mirror and reflects off. Some of that light goes into our eyes. When this happens, we can see our own bodies.

Common misconceptions

Light travels out from the eye to 'touch' the object.
It took a genius to show that light travels from a bright object, such as the Sun, to the object being seen and then to the eye (Ibn al-Haytham around the year 1000 CE).

We can see light travelling through space.
Light is only visible when it interacts with an object and is reflected into our eyes.

Progression

Key Stage	Development of ideas
EYFS	· Pupils can begin by noticing and describing different sources of light in their environment, including both natural (like the Sun) and artificial (like a lamp) light sources.
KS1 (ages 5-7)	· Pupils start learning about sources of light and the idea that darkness is the absence of light. This is a good time to introduce the concept of shadows as being what happens when light is blocked.
LKS2 (ages 7-9)	· Pupils can delve deeper into light, understanding how we see things (light bouncing off objects and into our eyes) and the concept of reflection.
UKS2 (ages 9-11)	· Pupils should learn how light behaves when it encounters different materials, leading to phenomena like reflection, refraction and absorption.
KS3 (ages 11-14)	· Pupils should deepen their understanding of light, including its speed, the spectrum of visible light, and complex phenomena such as the formation of rainbows, or the use of lenses.

Sound

The big idea of sound is that vibrations travel from a source (e.g. a drum), through a medium (e.g. the air), to the ear, where the vibrations are detected. The brain interprets the sound.

To make the most of this idea, expose pupils to many different ways of making sound. Let them investigate ways of changing the pitch and the volume of the sounds that they are producing. Pupils can experience vibrations in a variety of ways: feeling their throat as they hum, putting a tuning fork in water, or plucking a stringed instrument or stretched elastic band.

Pupils can understand sound using models and visualisations, such as the image below (animated versions can be found online).

The key problem with sound is that sound waves are invisible and difficult to measure. Models and diagrams are helpful to visualise sound waves travelling.

Representation of sound waves travelling.

Key questions

○ **How do you change the pitch of a sound?**
Pitch changes when an object, such as an elastic band, is stretched more tightly. The tighter it is, the faster it vibrates and the higher the pitch of the sound.

○ **How do you change the volume of a sound?**
The volume depends on how hard the object is struck, or plucked. If a drum is hit hard, it will be louder than if it is hit softly.

○ **Does sound only travel through air?**
Sounds can travel through any medium: gas, liquid or solid. Pupils can experience sound travelling through string (solid) using yoghurt cup telephones. They can understand that sound travels through water through the example of whale song.

○ **How do animals with lungs use them to produce sounds?**
To produce a sound, the air in the lungs is forced out through the animal's windpipe, which causes the air to vibrate and then travel out through either its mouth or nose. In humans, the windpipe contains vocal folds that allow control over the speed of the vibrations and more complex sounds to be made. To make a louder sound, the air is exhaled faster. The mouth is also used to shape the sound in speech, for example.

Common misconceptions

○ **Sound can only travel through air and not through solids and liquids.**
Sound can travel through solids, liquids or gases.

○ **Sounds can be produced without any objects being involved.**
All sounds need one or more objects to produce them – they are made by hitting, shaking, strumming, plucking or forcing air through an object to cause it to vibrate.

○ **If you hit an object harder, it will change the pitch of the sound produced.**
Hitting an object harder will increase the volume of the sound, but not the pitch.

○ **Sounds only travel in one direction from the source.**
Sound waves spread out as they move away from the source and can be heard in any direction. You can hear someone speaking even if you're standing behind them.

○ **High pitch sounds are loud and low pitch sounds are quiet.**
Pitch and volume are two completely separate things. High pitch sounds can be loud or quiet, and so can low pitch sounds.

Progression

Key Stage	Development of ideas
EYFS	· Pupils should start by exploring different sounds in their environment. They might play with musical instruments, listen to different types of music, or go on a 'sound walk' to identify different sounds.
KS1 (ages 5-7)	· Pupils should be able to identify how sounds are made, associating them with something vibrating. They should recognise that sounds get fainter as the distance from the sound source increases. They should begin to compare sounds (higher/lower, louder/quieter).
KS2 (ages 7-11)	· Pupils should be able to identify how sounds are made, recognising that vibrations from sounds travel through a medium to the ear. They should find patterns between the pitch of a sound and features of the object that produced it. They should also find patterns between the volume of a sound and the strength of the vibrations that produced it.
KS3 (ages 11-14)	· Pupils should learn about the properties of waves, including sound waves. This includes understanding that waves transfer energy and information without transferring matter. They should describe waves in terms of amplitude, wavelength, frequency and speed. They should also understand how sound waves can be reflected, refracted and absorbed.

Waves and vibrations

The big idea about waves and vibrations is that vibrations can cause waves and that sound and water waves cause backwards and forwards motion to travel from one place to another.

Waves can move through various substances, including water, air and solid materials.

Waves become very important at Key Stage 3 (ages 11-14) and onwards, so a solid foundation based on experience is important at primary school.

To make the most of this idea, conduct hands-on activities where pupils can see and feel vibrations and waves. For instance, creating ripples in a water tank, plucking a stretched rubber band and making a wave on a long rope can provide tangible experiences of waves and vibrations.

The key challenge in teaching about waves and vibrations is that, while they are integral to many experiences of the world, they often occur invisibly or imperceptibly. For instance, sound waves travelling through air, or seismic waves passing through the Earth, are not directly visible. Furthermore, concepts such as frequency, wavelength and amplitude involve abstract ideas and scientific vocabulary that can be challenging for pupils. Using visual aids, physical models and real-world examples can be effective in illustrating these concepts.

A diagram showing the direction of the wave's motion (right to left) and the motion of the duck (up and down).

Key questions

○ **What happens when you throw a stone into a pond?**
Can you describe the ripples? This question encourages pupils to think about waves and can serve as a starting point for a discussion about waves.

○ **How does sound travel from a guitar or whistle?**
How do you think the sound travels from there to your ears? This question introduces the concept of vibrations and sound waves.

○ **Can you think of other things that make waves when they vibrate?**
This question encourages pupils to make connections between vibrations and waves.

○ **What do you think will happen if we make our vibrations bigger or smaller?**
This question helps pupils start to think about amplitude, a key property of waves.

Common misconceptions

○ **Sound can travel in space.**
In reality, sound requires a medium (such as air, water, or a solid material) to travel. It can't travel through empty space, which is why astronauts can't hear each other without radios.

○ **Bigger waves always move faster.**
The size (amplitude) of a wave doesn't determine its speed. Wave speed is determined by the medium through which the wave is moving.

○ **Vibrations always produce sound.**
While vibrations can produce sound, not all vibrations lead to sound that we can hear. Some vibrations might be too fast, too slow, or too small for human ears to detect.

○ **All waves are similar to water waves.**
While water waves provide a good model, not all waves behave in the same way. For example, light waves can move through empty space, unlike water waves.

Progression

Key Stage	Development of ideas
EYFS	· Pupils can begin by noticing and feeling vibrations and seeing waves in their environment, such as when dropping a stone into water, or feeling the vibrations of a loud sound.
KS1 (ages 5-7)	· Pupils start learning about sound as a type of wave that we can hear. They can experience how sounds are made through vibrations and can be softer or louder based on the size of the vibration.
KS2 (ages 7-11)	· Pupils can begin to learn about other types of waves beyond sound, such as light and water waves.
KS3 (ages 11-14)	· Pupils should deepen their understanding of waves, studying more detailed properties such as frequency, wavelength and speed. They may also learn about the wide range of waves in the electromagnetic spectrum.

The solar system model

The big idea of the solar system model is to show how the planets orbit the Sun. To make the most of the solar system model, you should show that:

- the planets orbit the Sun;
- the further away from the Sun, the slower the planet travels; and
- the further away from the Sun, the further the planet has to travel to complete a full orbit.

The key problem with the solar system model is scale: if the Sun and planets were all to scale, the planets would need to be tiny and the distances between them would be huge. You can give a sense of this if you have a large playing field and a 1 m diameter ball to represent the Sun:

- Mercury would be a 3 mm ball 42 metres from the Sun;
- the Earth would be 9 mm in diameter and 108 metres from the Sun; and
- Neptune would be 35 mm in diameter and more than 3 kilometres from the Sun.

A classroom solar system model.

● Key questions

○ **Why does Neptune take the longest to travel around the Sun?**
It takes the longest because it has the furthest distance to travel and because it has the slowest speed of all of the planets.

○ **What is the difference between rotating and orbiting?**
An orbit is the path that an object travels through space (e.g. the Earth orbits the Sun). All objects in space rotate – they spin on their own axis. Some spin quickly and some spin very slowly.

○ **What evidence is there that the Sun is at the centre of the solar system?**
Galileo found two key pieces of evidence using his telescope:
- He saw moons orbiting Jupiter, which shows that smaller objects orbit bigger ones; and
- He saw the phases of Venus (it is a crescent sometimes and a full circle at other times). This happens because Venus orbits the Sun.

O **If we look at the sky, how can we tell if a bright object is a star or a planet?**
If you take photographs of the sky several days apart and then overlap the two photographs so that all the stars line up, you might see that one bright object has moved. This will be a planet.

Common misconceptions

O **The Sun is not a star.**
The Sun is a star – and quite an ordinary one too.

O **The solar system only includes the Sun, planets and our Moon.**
There are many other objects in our solar system, including asteroids, planetoids (like Pluto) and comets, as well as the space probes that humans have sent out.

O **The planets cannot be seen without a telescope.**
Jupiter and Venus are easy to see with our bare eyes. Mars and Saturn can also be seen unaided. Mercury is always close to the Sun, so it is harder to see, but it is possible. The others need a telescope to see them.

O **We have seasons because the Earth is closer to the Sun in the summer.**
This is similar to the misconception that the equator is warmer because it is closer to the Sun. The reason for both effects is the angle at which the Sun's rays fall on the Earth's surface.

Progression

Key Stage	Development of ideas
EYFS	· Pupils should know that there are stars and planets in space. Know that you need a rocket to get into space. Know that you need a spaceship to move from one planet to another.
KS1 (ages 5-7)	· Pupils should know that you need a special suit to survive in space. Know that people and robots can travel through space using rockets. Know that people have been to the Moon, but only robots have been to other planets.
LKS2 (ages 7-9)	· Pupils should use a solar system model to show how planets orbit the Sun and how moons orbit their planets. Pupils should know that the Sun is a star.
UKS2 (ages 9-11)	· Pupils should understand that the solar system model is not to scale – the planets are too small and the distances too big to make a convenient model. Pupils should know that the closer the planet is to the Sun, the faster it travels. · Pupils should be able to use a globe to explain day and night using the rotation of the Earth and be able to explain why the Sun appears to move across the sky over the course of a day.
KS3 (ages 11-14)	· Pupils will learn that gravity is the force that causes planets to orbit the Sun and moons their planets (without gravity, the planets would travel off into space in straight lines). They will calculate the weight of objects on different planets. They will learn about galaxies. They will finally learn about the role of the Earth's tilt in the seasons.

Circuits

The big idea of circuits is that charge needs a complete pathway (a circuit) to travel round. If there is a break in the pathway (an incomplete circuit), all of the charge stops moving.

To make the most of this idea, pupils need to experience real circuits and compare what they observe with physical models and diagrams.

The key problem with circuits is that the charge flowing is invisible: pupils need the support of models and diagrams to make sense of their experiences.

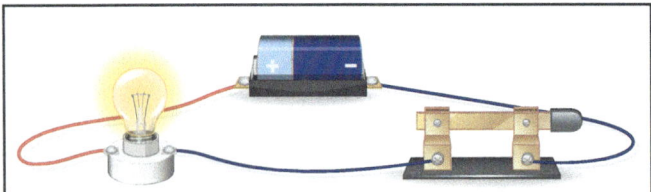 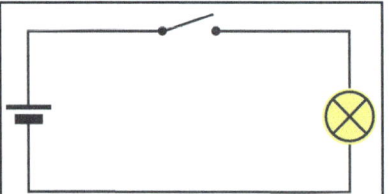

Comparing circuit diagrams at three different levels of abstraction.

Key questions

○ **Is this a complete circuit?**
Ask this question about real circuits and diagrams. Pupils need to understand that a break anywhere in the circuit will prevent the current flowing.

○ **Does it matter which side of the bulb you put the switch?**
It doesn't matter where you break the circuit – if the circuit isn't complete, the current will not flow.

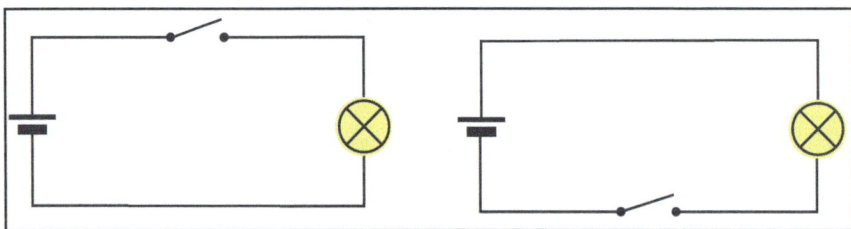

○ **How can you make the bulb brighter?**
You can add more cells.

● Common misconceptions

○ **The cell or battery provides the charge for a circuit.**
The charge is already in the wires and components: the cell just makes the charge move.

○ **You don't need a wire to carry the electricity back to the cell because the bulb uses up the electricity.**
The bulb doesn't use up electricity – the current needs a path to return to the cell.

○ **When we 'charge up' a battery, we are adding electrical charge.**
No charge is added to the battery. It is better to describe the cell as storing more energy.

● Progression

Key Stage	Development of ideas
EYFS & KS1 (ages 5-7)	· Pupils should learn that some everyday objects use electricity. They may have a battery or they may be plugged in.
LKS2 (ages 7-9)	· Pupils should be able to identify common appliances that run on electricity. · Pupils should be able to construct a simple series electrical circuit, identifying and naming its basic parts, including cells, wires, bulbs, switches and buzzers. · Pupils should be able to identify whether or not a lamp will light in a simple series circuit, based on whether or not the lamp is part of a complete loop with a battery. · Pupils should recognise that a switch opens and closes a circuit and associate this with whether or not a lamp lights in a simple series circuit. · Pupils should recognise some common conductors and insulators, and associate metals with being good conductors.
UKS2 (ages 9-11)	· Pupils should be able to associate the brightness of a lamp or the volume of a buzzer with the number and voltage of cells used in the circuit. · Pupils should be able to compare and give reasons for variations in how components function, including the brightness of bulbs, the loudness of buzzers and the on/off position of switches. · Pupils should use recognised symbols when representing a simple circuit in a diagram.
KS3 (ages 11-14)	· Pupils should learn about electric current, measured in amperes, in circuits, series and parallel circuits, currents. · Pupils should be able to add where branches meet and current as flow of charge. · Pupils should learn about potential difference, measured in volts, battery and bulb ratings; resistance, measured in ohms, as the ratio of potential difference (p.d.) to current. · Pupils should be able to identify differences in resistance between conducting and insulating components (quantitative).

Electrical conductors & insulators

The big idea about electrical conductors and insulators is that not all materials are alike when it comes to their interaction with electricity. Conductors are materials that allow electricity to pass through them easily, such as metals. On the other hand, insulators are materials that resist or block the flow of electricity, such as rubber or plastic.

To make the most of this idea, you should provide practical examples and hands-on activities. A simple circuit-building activity, where pupils test different materials (e.g. a coin, plastic toy, rubber band, piece of wood) to see if they complete the circuit, can be very effective. This allows pupils to see first-hand which materials conduct electricity and which don't. It's crucial to emphasise safety precautions when dealing with electricity, to avoid any mishaps.

The key problem in teaching electrical conductors and insulators is that the flow of electricity isn't something that we can see directly. This can make it difficult for pupils to grasp the idea of how electricity travels. Overcome this challenge by using diagrams to illustrate how electricity flows and explaining that conductors and insulators control that flow. Tools such as light bulbs in circuits can also provide a visible indication of whether electricity is passing through a material or not.

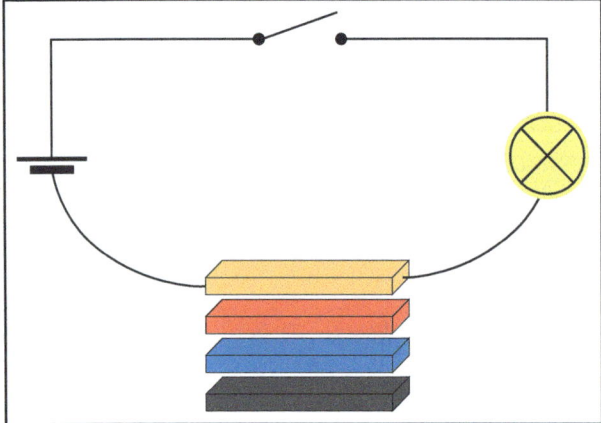

Conductor	Insulator
Steel	Plastic
Aluminium	Cardboard

A circuit to check whether a substance is an electrical insulator or conductor.

Key questions

O **What do you think will happen if we make a metal spoon part of our circuit?**
What about a plastic spoon? These questions prompt pupils to apply their understanding of electrical conductors and insulators and to predict outcomes.

O **Why do you think the wires in electrical appliances are covered in plastic?**
This question encourages pupils to think about the practical applications of insulators and safety considerations in everyday life. It checks that pupils understand that, inside the plastic coating, there is metal wire. The colours of the wire make no difference to the circuit.

○ **Can you explain why our light bulb isn't lighting up in our circuit?**
This question can lead to discussions about the completeness of a circuit and the role of conductors in allowing electricity to flow.

● Common misconceptions

○ **All metals are conductors, and all non-metals are insulators.**
Most metals are good conductors of electricity and many non-metals are insulators. However, some non-metals, such as graphite (a form of carbon), can conduct electricity.

○ **Electric current is used up as it passes through a circuit.**
Electric current is not used up; instead, it is the energy that the current carries that is transferred or transformed in electrical devices.

○ **Electricity only flows through conductors.**
Electricity can pass through both conductors and insulators, but it does so much more easily through conductors. Insulators greatly resist the flow of electricity but, under certain conditions (like very high voltage), electricity can still pass through them.

○ **Wires are made of plastic (because you can usually only see the plastic coating).**
Wires are always made of a conducting material (typically copper) with an insulating coating. The colour of the plastic makes no difference to the circuit, but might be helpful to a person trying to understand the circuit.

● Progression

Key Stage	Development of ideas
EYFS	· Pupils are encouraged to experience and discuss the world around them. Although the concepts of conductors and insulators are not directly introduced, they can be involved in discussion in context about electricity and safety.
KS1 (ages 5-7)	· Pupils should observe and discuss everyday uses of different materials, which could include a conversation about why certain materials are used for electrical wiring and others for insulating wires.
LKS2 (ages 7-9)	· Pupils start to learn about electricity, creating simple circuits and understanding that a switch opens and closes a circuit. They can test whether or not a lamp will light in a simple series circuit based on whether or not the lamp is part of a complete loop with a battery.
UKS2 (ages 9-11)	· Pupils should construct simple series circuits, and investigate what happens when they try different components, including switches and bulbs. They can also explore which materials conduct electricity, noting patterns and classifying objects into those that are electrical conductors and those that are insulators.
KS3 (ages 11-14)	· Pupils should learn further how electricity works, including how voltage and resistance in a circuit are related to the flow of electrical charge. They can investigate the varying effectiveness of different materials as conductors and insulators in more depth.

Charge and current

The big idea of charge is that when charged objects interact with other charged objects, they **attract** or **repel**. The big idea of current is that current is moving charge.

To make the most of this idea, provide pupils with many clear examples of charged objects, such as rubbed balloons, combs and rulers, and observe their effects. When pupils are confident talking about charge, you can introduce the idea of current as the movement of charges.

The key problem with charge and current is that they are both abstract. You cannot see charge, but only see its effects (attracting and repelling other charged objects). Current is the movement of charges – you cannot see current in a circuit, but only observe its effects (e.g. a bulb lights, or a buzzer buzzes).

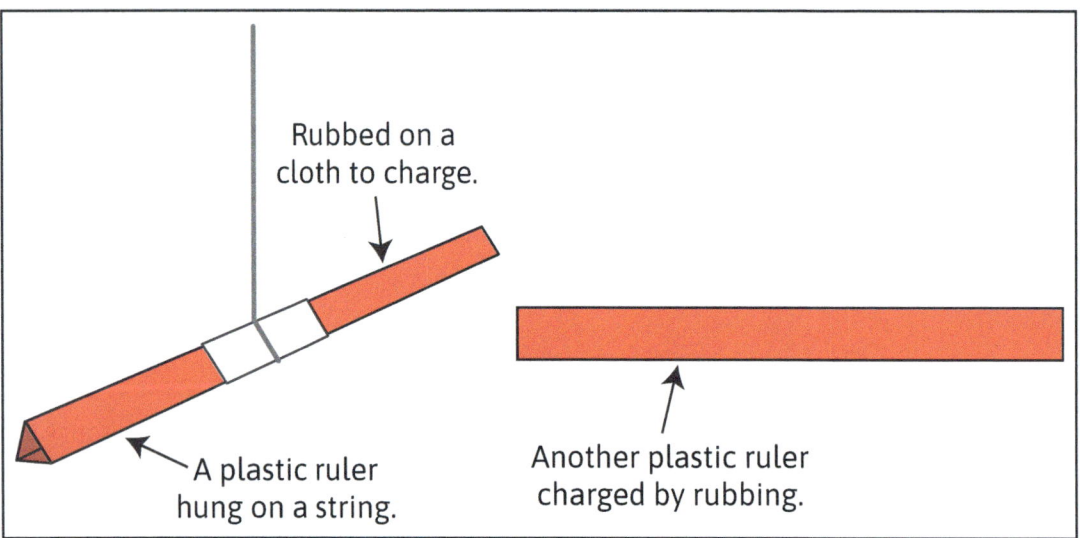

Rubbed on a cloth to charge.

A plastic ruler hung on a string.

Another plastic ruler charged by rubbing.

Like charges repel. Opposite charges attract.

Key questions

○ **Where does the charge come from in a circuit?**
The charge is already in the circuit, but it doesn't move until you connect it to a cell or battery.

○ **Why do we sometimes talk about charges (e.g. electrons) and other times talk about charge?**
Some particles are charged (for example, electrons). When these particles move, we have a current. The charges that move through wires are electrons. (Only try to explain this if a pupil asks.)

Common misconceptions

○ **The cell or battery provides the charge for a circuit.**
The charge is already in the wires and components: the cell just makes the charge move.

Progression

Key Stage	Development of ideas
EYFS	· Pupils should know that many electrical appliances use electricity.
KS1 (ages 5-7)	· Pupils should know that some electrical appliances are plugged in, while others use batteries. Some batteries can be 'charged'.
LKS2 (ages 7-9)	· Pupils should experience charged objects and their effects. Charge a balloon and let it stick to the wall; pick up small pieces of paper and pieces of foil. Rub the balloon on hair and watch it attract the hair. Charged balloons will be attracted to jumpers and other materials.
UKS2 (ages 9-11)	· Pupil should be able to show that charges attract and repel. · Pupil should know that current is charge moving. Use a model (e.g. the **rope current model** on page 82) to show how charge flows around a circuit as a current.
KS3 (ages 11-14)	· Pupils should be able to measure electric current, measured in amperes in series and parallel circuits using ammeters. · Pupils should understand charging objects as the transfer of electrons. · Pupil should know that the electric field exists in the space between charged objects not in contact.

The 'rope' circuit model

The big idea of a circuit model is that it helps pupils to understand what is happening in a circuit. There are many simple models to help understand electric current. The rope model is very effective for modelling current in a series circuit.

In this model:

- The rope is the charge. This helps pupils to understand that the charge is already in the wire and not provided by the battery.
- The battery or cell moves the rope. This shows that the battery or cell moves the charge.
- The rope doesn't get used up by the bulbs. This helps pupils to understand that the charge doesn't get used up by the bulbs.
- The rope moves at the same speed all around the circuit. This helps show that the current is the same all the way around the circuit.
- The pupils represent the wires. Point out that the wires don't move, but the charge does.

The rope model in action.

The key problem with using models is knowing how to apply them to real life. The rope model is great for visualising how charge flows round a series circuit, but it doesn't work for parallel circuits.

● Key questions

○ **What happens when the cell stops pushing the rope (charge) round?**
The rope stops moving.

○ **How could you make the bulbs light up more brightly?**
Make the rope (charge) move more quickly – you could do this by adding anther cell.

○ **How could you represent a switch in the circuit?**
A switch stops the charge moving. You could show this by grabbing hold of the rope to stop it moving. It doesn't matter where in the circuit you grab it – it all stops.

● Common misconceptions

○ Pupils may struggle to match each element of the model to real life.

○ Pupils who are acting as the wires may push the rope around (in fact, they should be providing **resistance** to the flow of charge.

○ Pupils may use the words 'battery' and 'cell' interchangeably. One pupil should be used to represent one **cell**. You can model a battery by making two or more pupils be cells.

○ Pupils may not realise that the more bulbs you have in the circuit, the slower the rope (charges) should move – and the dimmer each bulb should be.

○ Pupils may not realise that the more cells you have in the circuit, the faster the rope (charge) should move – and the brighter the bulbs should be.

● Progression

Key Stage	Development of ideas
KS1 (ages 5-7)	· Pupils are introduced to the idea of electricity and its uses. They might create simple circuits using batteries, wires and bulbs. They can be introduced to the idea that a complete path is needed for the bulb to light up, using analogies such as a closed loop or circle.
LKS2 (ages 7-9)	· Pupils can start to use series circuits with multiple components, understanding the roles of each (e.g. switches). They can also begin to experiment with insulators and conductors.
UKS2 (ages 9-11)	· Pupils can begin to use circuit symbols and use more models to understand what is happening in a circuit.
KS3 (ages 11-14)	· Pupils should be familiar with conventional symbols for drawing circuit diagrams. They can use more advanced models to understand series and parallel circuits. They will build on their understanding of current and charge and introduce the idea of voltage and resistance.

Energy

The big idea of energy is that it is a **conserved quantity** (the total amount of energy stored by a system does not change); however, it is not the **cause** of anything: it is generally unhelpful to use the term 'energy' in an explanation of **why** something happens.

To make the most of **energy** as an analytical tool, it is best to avoid using it unless you are going to do an energy analysis! So, try to avoid invoking it as a generalised explanatory flourish. It is more helpful to explain phenomena using mechanisms and processes that involve tangible items, such as balls, blocks, particles, identifiable substances (such as sugar, carbon dioxide, oxygen) and other measurable quantities such as temperature, force or mass.

The idea of energy is useful for doing calculations, because it is conserved. If it looks like the quantity of energy has increased or decreased, you have simply forgotten to account for it elsewhere.

The challenge with discussing energy with young people is that the word is used in everyday life, in adverts, books and on TV, and its meaning in those situations rarely conforms to the scientific meaning. This can lead to misconceptions, but it isn't anyone's fault: it's just that scientists use the word differently from everyone else.

Energy is not taught as a topic in the primary science National Curriculum, so you don't need to use the word in science lessons at all but, if you do, you could try rephrasing the sentence (see the examples below).

If someone says...	You could say...	Comment
Sports drinks give you energy.	Sports drinks provide your muscles with the sugars that they need to move.	The original sentence suggests that energy is a substance. Better to rephrase using actual substances.
The leaves absorb energy from the Sun.	The leaves absorb sunlight.	This sentence also suggests that energy is a substance. This time, the leaf is absorbing light.

Wind turbines generate energy.	Wind turbines use the wind to generate electricity.	Words such as 'generate' suggest to pupils that energy can be made. Better to say what is actually being generated – electricity.
Your muscles use up energy when you run.	Your muscles use up sugar and oxygen when you run.	Phrases such as 'use up' suggest to pupils that energy can be destroyed. Better to say what is actually being used up.

Key questions

- **What is really being absorbed?**
  It might be light, infra-red radiation, sound, or something else. Unlike energy, all these have some physical identity.

- **What really makes something happen?**
  It is usually a difference – of temperature, pressure, concentration, or forces.

- **What is really being 'used up' here?**
  It might be a physical substance, such as sugar or petrol.

- **What is really being 'created' here?**
  It might be a quantity such as electricity in a generator, or sugar during photosynthesis.

Common misconceptions

- **Energy is created during photosynthesis.**
  It is sugar that is being created.

- **Energy is 'used up' when we leave a light on, exercise or drive a car.**
  It is a fuel (at a power station), sugar, or petrol that is being used up.

Progression

Context	EYFS/KS1	KS2	KS3
Food	· Our bodies need food and oxygen to move and keep warm.	· When you eat food, you are putting carbohydrates/ sugars into your body. Your body uses these chemicals (in a reaction with oxygen) to move about, keep warm and to grow.	· Energy is stored chemically by the food (plus oxygen). After (or during) an activity, the energy is stored differently: either thermally or kinetically.
Photosynthesis	· Plants use sunlight to make their food. They need food to grow.	· Light arrives from the Sun, which plants can use to make food.	· The Sun is the original source of energy for all life on Earth. When the energy stored by a plant increases, the energy stored by the Sun has decreased.
Fuel	· A car needs petrol (and oxygen) to move.	· A car moves because it burns a fuel in oxygen (in a controlled way). There is a limit to how far or fast it can go, and that is determined by how much energy is stored chemically by the fuel (plus oxygen).	· Fossil fuels store a lot of energy chemically (as long as there is oxygen available). They can be burned to do useful jobs for us (keep us warm and make things move). Once they have been burned, the energy is stored in less useful ways and can no longer do jobs for us. It is helpful to know how much energy fossil fuels store so that we can work out how much we need to do certain jobs – or how long they are going to last as a global resource.
We put batteries and cells in phones	· A phone needs a charged battery to work. Over time, a battery goes flat and needs to be recharged.	· We charge a phone's battery using electricity.	· A battery stores energy chemically. When we charge it, we are topping up its store. An energy store somewhere else (a power station, the Sun, etc) has been depleted by the same amount.
Alternative Energy Sources	· The wind makes the windmill turn.	· The wind makes the windmill turn to generate electricity.	· We can use a windmill to do useful jobs for us – even charge up a battery. The energy store that has been depleted to make the wind blow is the Sun.

At Key Stage 3, pupils are taught about energy stores.

A fast-moving object stores energy due to its **movement** (we say that 'the energy is stored kinetically' or 'there is a kinetic store of energy associated with the moving object').

A fully-charged battery stores energy due to the chemicals that it contains (which can react and drive an electric current); we say that 'it stores energy chemically' or 'there is energy in its **chemical store**'.

A child at the top of a zip-wire stores energy because she is high up (and the Earth's gravity is pulling her down); the system stores energy because of gravity. We say that it is 'storing energy gravitationally' or there is energy in its **gravitational store**.

A hot cup of tea stores energy because of its high temperature; we say that 'it is storing energy thermally' or there is 'energy in its **thermal store**'.

Pupils also begin to use energy in calculations: the additional energy stored thermally by a cup of tea might be 60,000 joules. This tells us two things. First, we needed to use up 60,000 joules, worth of a fuel in order to make that cup of tea. Secondly, when the tea cools, that 60,000 joules has not disappeared, but will be stored thermally by the surroundings. However, the slightly warmer surroundings are not as useful a store of energy as the original fuel that was burned to boil the water for the tea.

How we can protect the environment

The big idea about protecting the environment is that even small actions can make a difference. Locally, that means looking after our parks, not littering, and reducing, reusing and recycling waste. Globally, it involves understanding the impact of climate change and working towards reducing our carbon footprint.

To make the most of this idea, you should first help your pupils to understand what the environment is and why it's essential. From there, break down the concept of protecting the environment into manageable, relatable pieces. Start with actions that they can do in their homes and school, such as recycling and composting. Then extend it to the local community by organising activities such as tree-planting, litter-picking, or visits to local recycling plants. Gradually build up to broader topics like global warming, deforestation and ocean pollution and, where possible, tie it back to the choices that they can make in their daily lives.

The key problem with teaching environmental protection is its complexity and scale. Moreover, environmental issues can often feel overwhelming and disheartening, especially when it comes to the larger problems such as climate change. Emphasise hope and the difference that individual and collective actions can make.

● Key questions

○ **What do you think would happen if we didn't clean up litter in our community?**
Our neighbourhood would become dirty, and it could be harmful to animals. It might also lead to diseases.

○ **Can you tell me what recycling is and why it's important?**
Recycling is when we take things that are used and process them to make new items. It's important because it helps to save resources and reduces the amount of waste that we produce.

○ **What are some ways in which we can save water at home?**
We can turn off the tap while brushing our teeth, spend less time in the shower and not use a hose to water the garden.

○ **Can you think of ways that we can reduce the amount of electricity we use?**
We can turn off lights when we leave a room, unplug devices when not in use, and use energy-efficient appliances.

○ **How do you think what we do locally might impact the environment globally?**
If we recycle locally, we can reduce the amount of waste that ends up in landfills. If we use the car less, there will be less carbon dioxide in the air. If we use water more carefully, we won't have as much drought.

○ **How do you think the things that we buy might impact the environment?**
If we buy a lot of plastic things, this creates more waste. But if we choose things with less packaging, or made from recycled materials, it's better for the environment.

○ **Why do you think some people find it hard to recycle or save energy?**
Maybe they don't understand why it's important, or they might find it inconvenient. It can cost more at first to insulate your house, for example.

Common misconceptions

○ **My individual actions won't make a difference.**
Many people believe that environmental issues are too large for one person's actions to have any meaningful impact. In reality, collective small actions by individuals can lead to significant changes. For example, if everyone decided to reduce their meat consumption, or choose public transportation over private cars, the impact would be substantial.

○ **Recycling is the only solution to waste.**
While recycling is a crucial part of managing waste, it is not the only solution.

○ **The emphasis should be on the first two R's: Reduce and Reuse.**
We need to reduce our consumption and waste generation and reuse items as much as possible, before turning to recycling.

○ **All plastics are recyclable.**
Not all plastics can be recycled, and the ones that can often require specific facilities to do so. Additionally, each time that plastic is recycled, its quality decreases. It's essential to minimise our use of single-use plastics and choose reusable alternatives.

○ **Climate change is only about warming temperatures.**
While global warming is a significant aspect of climate change, it also includes changes in weather patterns, rising sea levels, and increasing frequency and intensity of extreme weather events.

Progression

Key Stage	Development of ideas
EYFS	· Pupils should learn about the world around them through exploration, discussion and simple observations. The concept of protecting the environment can be introduced through practical activities such as recycling or gardening.
KS1 (ages 5-7)	· Pupils can start learning about the importance of taking care of their environment, for instance, not littering, turning off lights when you leave the room, recycling and reducing the number of short trips in cars.
LKS2 (ages 7-9)	· Pupils should learn about the damaging effects of human activity on the environment, and they might begin learning about conservation. They should also learn how environments can change as a result of human actions.
UKS2 (ages 9-11)	· Pupils should learn about how living things and their environment can be affected by human activity and how changes could lead to the endangerment of specific species. They might also learn different ways in which individuals and societies can work to reduce negative impacts and contribute positively to the environment.
KS3 (ages 11-14)	· Pupils should learn about more complex environmental issues, including the production of carbon dioxide by human activity and the impact on climate. They should understand how human and physical processes interact to influence and change environments and climates.

Global warming

The big idea about global warming is that human activities are increasing the Earth's average temperature. This is primarily due to the release of greenhouse gases like carbon dioxide and methane, which trap heat from the Sun in the Earth's atmosphere. Global warming influences weather patterns, sea levels and ecosystems.

To make the most of this idea, relate global warming to everyday experiences and future implications. Discuss how changes in local weather patterns, shifts in seasons, or changes in local wildlife might be connected to global warming. Use concrete examples of human activities that contribute to greenhouse gas emissions, such as burning fossil fuels for transport or electricity.

The key challenge in teaching about global warming is the abstract nature of the greenhouse effect, as well as the scale of its impacts. Pupils often find it difficult to understand how invisible gases can trap heat, or how small changes in average temperatures can lead to dramatic changes in climate. Diagrams and analogies (e.g. visiting a greenhouse) can help to explain these ideas.

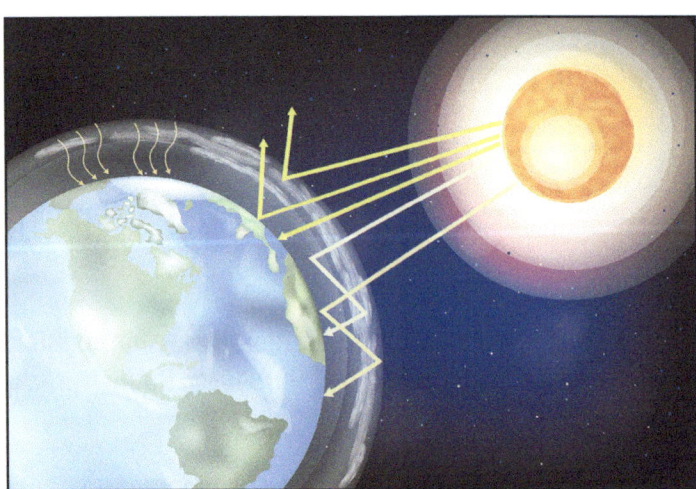

The atmosphere traps some heat, but some still escapes into space. To stay at a steady temperature, the heat lost must balance the heat gained from the Sun.

● Key questions

○ **What do you understand by the term 'global warming'?**
Global warming is when the Earth gets hotter because of gases like carbon dioxide that people release into the air.

○ **How do you think global warming affects our planet?**
It can make the weather more extreme, with hotter summers and colder winters. It also makes the sea levels rise, which can cause flooding.

○ **How might global warming affect the animals and plants around us?**
Some animals and plants might not be able to survive if it gets too hot, or if their habitat changes too much because of the weather.

○ **How does global warming impact the weather?**
Global warming can lead to more extreme weather such as heatwaves, heavy rain and snowfall, or even droughts.

○ **Can you name some human activities that contribute to global warming?**
Driving cars, burning coal for electricity, and cutting down forests are all things that can cause global warming.

○ **What are some things that we can do at home or school to reduce global warming?**
We can turn off lights when we leave a room, recycle and compost our waste, walk or ride to school, and plant trees.

○ **Why do you think that some people don't believe in global warming?**
They might not understand the science, or they might find it hard to believe that humans can change the Earth's climate.

Common misconceptions

○ **Global warming and the ozone hole are the same problem.**
While both are environmental issues related to the atmosphere, they are separate problems with different causes.

○ **If it's cold outside, global warming must be wrong.**
This confusion stems from misunderstanding the difference between weather (short-term, local conditions) and climate (long-term patterns).

○ **Not all scientists agree about global warming.**
While individual opinions vary, the overwhelming majority of climate scientists agree that global warming is happening and is primarily caused by human activities.

○ **Global warming only affects polar bears and ice caps.**
Global warming has diverse effects across the planet, influencing weather patterns, sea levels, agriculture and ecosystems everywhere, not just in polar regions.

Progression

Key Stage	Development of ideas
EYFS	· Pupils can begin to understand the basics of weather and seasonal changes, laying the foundation for later understanding of more complex climate concepts.
KS1 (ages 5-7)	· Pupils start learning about daily and seasonal weather patterns in the UK. This could introduce the idea that climate can change over time.
LKS2 (ages 7-9)	· Pupils should start to understand the key aspects of human geography, which can include the influence of human activity on the environment.
UKS2 (ages 9-11)	· Pupils should have the opportunity to experience a more in-depth study of climate zones around the world, and a basic introduction to how human activities can influence climate.
KS3 (ages 11-14)	· Pupils should deepen their understanding of the interaction between human and physical geography, including how human activities contribute to global warming and its effects on different systems of the Earth.

Climate change

The big idea about climate change is that it involves long-term changes in temperature and weather patterns in a place. Climate change is primarily driven by human activities, especially the burning of fossil fuels such as coal, oil and gas, which increases the concentration of greenhouse gases in the Earth's atmosphere and warms the planet. Climate change includes global warming, but also the impacts of global warming, such as weather changes and other environmental changes such as deforestation.

To make the most of this idea, encourage pupils to investigate the impacts of climate change locally and globally, and to consider the actions that they can take to mitigate climate change. Real-world examples, such as the changing seasons or extreme weather events, can make these concepts more tangible for pupils.

The key challenge in teaching about climate change lies in its complexity and scale. The mechanisms driving climate change involve many different processes and systems – from atmospheric science to energy production to economics. Furthermore, the effects of climate change are wide-ranging and long-term, making them difficult to observe directly in the short term. Using images, models and case studies can help to explain these concepts and show the impacts of and solutions to climate change.

● Key questions

○ **What do you understand by the term 'climate change'?**
Climate change means the long-term changes in temperature, rainfall, wind, and all other aspects of the Earth's climate. It is getting warmer in many places and this affects the weather.

○ **How do you think climate change affects our planet?**
Climate change can cause more extreme weather events such as storms, floods and droughts. It can also make sea levels rise, which could cause problems for people living near the coast.

○ **What is the difference between climate and weather?**
Weather is the condition of the atmosphere over a short period of time, and climate is how the atmosphere 'behaves' over relatively long periods of time (usually 30 years or more).

○ **Can you name some human activities that contribute to climate change?**
Burning fossil fuels like coal, oil and gas for energy, cutting down trees and driving cars can all contribute to climate change.

○ **How might climate change affect the animals and plants around us?**
Some animals and plants might not be able to survive if their habitat changes too much because of climate change. For example, polar bears need ice to live on, and it's melting because of the warmer climate.

Common misconceptions

○ **Climate change and global warming are the same.**
While related, these terms refer to different things. Global warming is the long-term heating of Earth's climate system, while climate change includes global warming, but also other changes such as sea level rise, ice mass loss and shifts in weather patterns.

○ **Weather events can prove or disprove climate change.**
Weather is what we experience in the short term, while climate is the long-term average of weather patterns. An unusually cold day doesn't mean global warming isn't happening.

○ **Climate has always been changing; humans are not responsible.**
While it's true that Earth's climate has changed throughout its history, the current rate of change is much faster than most past changes, and scientists have linked this directly to human activities.

○ **All effects of climate change are in the future.**
Some effects of climate change are already happening, including increased frequency and intensity of some extreme weather events, rising sea levels and changes in ecosystems.

Progression

Key Stage	Development of ideas
EYFS	· Pupils can begin by understanding the basic concept of weather and seasonal changes.
KS1 (ages 5-7)	· Pupils start learning about the different types of weather and how it changes over time. They can also start to understand the basic human activities that impact the environment.
LKS2 (ages 7-9)	· Pupils can delve deeper into the concept of climate and understand the differences between weather and climate. They can also learn more about how human activities can affect the natural world.
UKS2 (ages 9-11)	· Pupils can learn about the role of greenhouse gases and how human activities contribute to their increase. This stage may involve a more detailed exploration of climate change, its causes and effects.
KS3 (ages 11-14)	· Pupils should deepen their understanding of climate change, including the scientific evidence for it, its potential impacts and mitigation strategies. This can involve learning about the carbon cycle, renewable energy sources and global climate policies.

Carbon dioxide & oxygen

The big idea about oxygen and carbon dioxide is that they are essential gases in the Earth's atmosphere, playing vital roles in the process of life. Oxygen (O_2) is a gas that all living things (including plants) use to respire (see the **Respiration** chapter). Oxygen is also essential for burning.

Carbon dioxide (CO_2), on the other hand, is a gas that plants use during photosynthesis to make food, using sunlight. Animals breathe out carbon dioxide when they exhale. Burning produced carbon dioxide.

The key problem in teaching about oxygen and carbon dioxide to primary school pupils lies in the abstract nature of gases. Young pupils often find it challenging to understand something that they cannot see or touch.

The biggest part of our atmosphere is nitrogen (N_2), which makes up almost 4/5 of the air that we breathe. Oxygen makes up around 1/5. So where is the carbon dioxide? Even though carbon dioxide plays such a big role in our bodies and environment, it only makes up 0.04% of our atmosphere. Even when we breathe out, our breath still only consists of 4% CO_2.

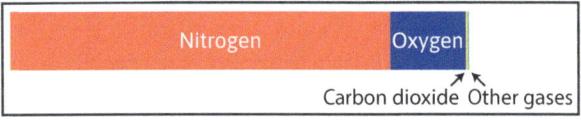

The composition of the Earth's atmosphere (Note: carbon dioxide is a very small component (around 0.04%)).

Key questions

○ **What is carbon dioxide and how can it be produced?**
Carbon dioxide is a gas. It can be produced by natural processes, such as respiration and by volcanoes. It can also be made when we burn fossil fuels.

○ **How do plants and animals use carbon dioxide and oxygen?**
Plants use carbon dioxide to make food (through photosynthesis). All living things (plants and animals) use oxygen to respire.

○ **Is there always the same amount of carbon dioxide in the atmosphere?**
The amount of carbon dioxide in the atmosphere can change naturally (through volcanoes and natural climate change), but this usually takes a very long time and the changes are small. Over the last century, however, humans have increased the amount of carbon dioxide in the atmosphere at a much higher rate.

Common misconceptions

○ **Many people use the word air and oxygen interchangeably.**
However, air contains just 21% oxygen. Most of the rest is nitrogen.

○ **Most people overestimate the concentration of carbon dioxide in the atmosphere.**
The percentage of CO_2 is tiny, but even a small increase has a large impact on our climate.

- **Many people believe that burning fossil fuels is using up the oxygen that we need to breathe.** It is true that burning fossil fuels reduces the concentration of oxygen in the atmosphere, but only by incredibly small amounts.

- **Many people believe that deforestation reduces the amount of oxygen we will have in the air.** Oxygen levels are falling, but incredibly slowly. In the last million years, it has fallen from 22% to 21%. This doesn't appear to be causing a problem for life on Earth.

Carbon dioxide and the environment

In the last 200 years, the concentration of carbon dioxide in the atmosphere has increased from below 0.03% to 0.04% – this is a huge change. Even very small amounts of carbon dioxide in the atmosphere make a big difference.

During the last Ice Age, the concentration of carbon dioxide dropped below 0.02%. Now that the concentration is 0.04%, we have record temperatures in the Arctic and wildfires across the globe.

This chart shows how significantly and how rapidly the concentration of carbon dioxide is changing.

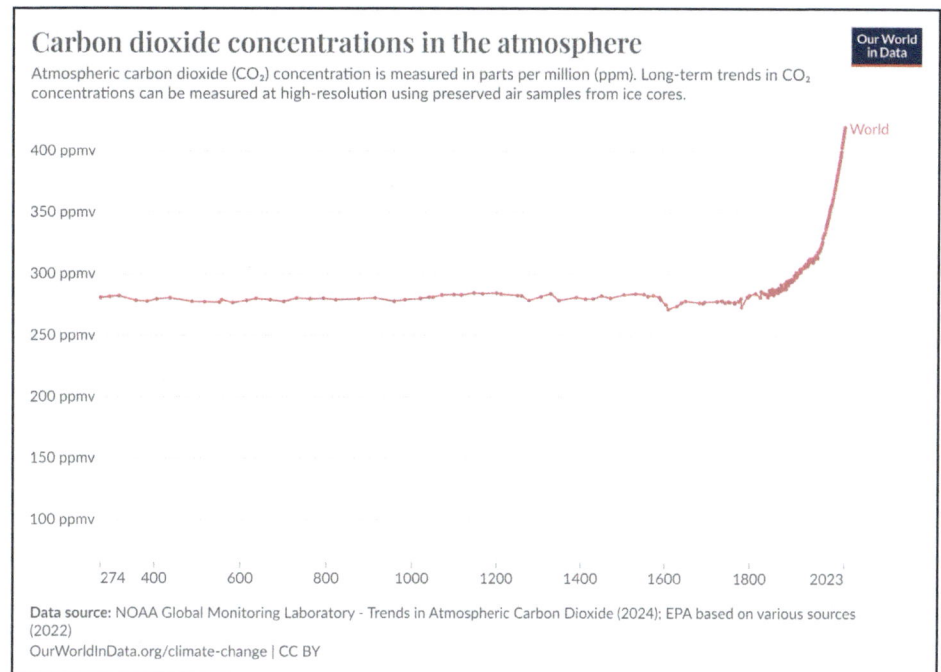

Carbon dioxide concentrations in the atmosphere

Atmospheric carbon dioxide (CO_2) concentration is measured in parts per million (ppm). Long-term trends in CO_2 concentrations can be measured at high-resolution using preserved air samples from ice cores.

Data source: NOAA Global Monitoring Laboratory - Trends in Atmospheric Carbon Dioxide (2024); EPA based on various sources (2022)
OurWorldInData.org/climate-change | CC BY

Progression

Key Stage	Development of ideas
EYFS	· Pupils might begin to learn about air and breathing through simple observations and activities.
KS1 (ages 5-7)	· Pupils might start learning about the needs of animals, including humans, to survive (such as the need for air to breathe). However, the distinction between oxygen and carbon dioxide may not be detailed at this stage.
LKS2 (ages 7-9)	· Pupils should learn about the function of different parts of plants, possibly including that leaves take in air. They might also discuss the role of breathing in animals. This lays the groundwork for understanding the role of oxygen in respiration and carbon dioxide in photosynthesis.
UKS2 (ages 9-11)	· Pupils should learn about the process of photosynthesis, including the fact that plants take in carbon dioxide and release oxygen. They might also learn about human respiration, understanding that humans take in oxygen and release carbon dioxide.
KS3 (ages 11-14)	· Pupils should delve deeper into the properties and roles of oxygen and carbon dioxide. This includes understanding the chemical reactions involved in photosynthesis and respiration, the role of oxygen in combustion, and how carbon dioxide contributes to the greenhouse effect and climate change.

The carbon cycle

The big idea about the carbon cycle is that the element carbon, which is essential to all life on Earth, is constantly recycled through the Earth's ecosystem.

The carbon cycle involves various stages, including photosynthesis, respiration, decomposition and fossilisation. Through these stages, carbon moves between the atmosphere, oceans, soil and living organisms, ensuring that this essential element is always available in the various forms needed for life to thrive.

To make the most of this idea, you should break down the complex process into its individual stages and relate it to everyday examples. At primary school level, the key stages of the carbon cycle are that:

1. Plants take in carbon dioxide from the air in order to use the carbon for growth, reproduction and repair.
2. Animals obtain the carbon that they need through eating plants or other animals.
3. Carbon dioxide is released back into the atmosphere through respiration.

As pupils progress, they learn that carbon is a key element in soils when leaves fall to the ground and decompose, and how carbon can become trapped underground as fossil fuels. This may lead to them to learn how carbon absorbed by a prehistoric plant can be released back into the atmosphere as we burn fossil fuels.

The key problem in teaching the carbon cycle is its abstract nature, coupled with the integration of various scientific disciplines such as biology, chemistry and environmental science. Young pupils may find it challenging to visualise and connect the different stages of the carbon cycle, especially as they might not yet have a strong foundation in these scientific areas.

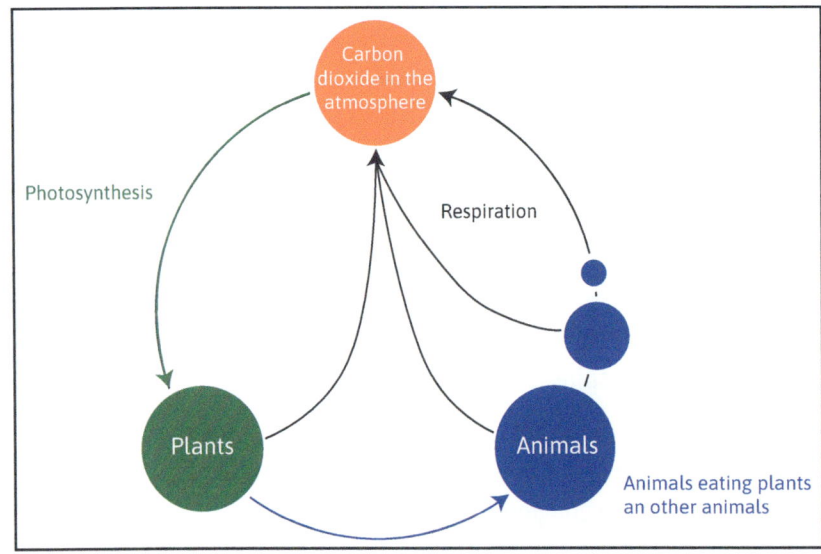

The key elements of the carbon cycle.

It is important to note that every plant and animal in the cycle releases carbon dioxide straight into the atmosphere through respiration.

● Key questions

○ **Is the carbon cycle good or bad for the planet?**
All life on the planet depends on the carbon cycle, so it is good! However, burning fossil fuels is also part of the carbon cycle.

○ **What happens to the carbon cycle when deforestation takes place?**
The amount of CO_2 in the atmosphere increases and can lead to global warming.

○ **What happens to the carbon cycle when we burn fossil fuels?**
The amount of CO_2 in the atmosphere increases and can lead to global warming.

● Common misconceptions

○ **Plants don't respire and produce carbon dioxide.**
Plants respire and produce carbon dioxide (CO_2).

○ **Deforestation leads to reduced oxygen in the atmosphere.**
Although this is technically true, the amount of oxygen decrease is barely detectable. The increase in carbon dioxide is the real problem.

○ **Carbon dioxide in the atmosphere is a bad thing.**
Without carbon dioxide, plants would not be able to grow. We also benefit from the natural greenhouse effect (it is the enhanced greenhouse effect that is causing problems).

○ **Humans cause the carbon cycle by burning fossil fuels.**
The carbon cycle has existed as long as there has been life on the planet.

● Progression

Key Stage	Development of ideas
EYFS	· Pupils can begin to learn about plants and how they grow, including understanding that plants need air, light, water and soil.
KS1 (ages 5-7)	· Pupils should learn about plants and animals and understand that they are alive and grow. This lays the groundwork for later understanding of the carbon cycle.
LKS2 (ages 7-9)	· Pupils should learn about the relationship between living things and their environment. They might begin to understand how plants and animals depend on each other, paving the way for a deeper understanding of ecological relationships – this supports a later understanding of the carbon cycle.
UKS2 (ages 9-11)	· Pupils should learn about the process of photosynthesis and how plants create food using sunlight and carbon dioxide. Although the carbon cycle might not be explicitly taught, this begins to introduce key components.
KS3 (ages 11-14)	· Pupils should delve into the carbon cycle in more detail. They will learn how carbon is cycled through the atmosphere, oceans and organisms, understanding key processes such as respiration, photosynthesis, decomposition and combustion. They should also discuss the role of human activities in altering the carbon cycle, particularly in the context of climate change.

The water cycle

The big idea about the water cycle is that it is a continuous process by which water moves through the environment. The cycle involves several key stages: **evaporation** (water changing from liquid to gas), **condensation** (water vapour cooling to form droplets), **precipitation** (water droplets combining to form rain, snow, etc. that falls to the Earth), and **collection** (water pooling in bodies of water and being absorbed into the ground).

To make the most of this idea, you should try to connect it with real-world examples and observations. For instance, discuss how a puddle disappears after a sunny day (evaporation), or how dew forms on grass (condensation). You can also conduct simple models such as creating a mini water cycle in a plastic bag (leave the model on a windowsill and make observations over the course of several days).

The key problem in teaching about the water cycle is that it's a process that takes place on a global scale and over a long period of time, which can be hard for pupils to grasp. Additionally, the concepts of evaporation and condensation can be challenging, as they involve changes in state that aren't easily observable. To overcome this, break down the cycle into individual stages and explain each in detail, with demonstrations or experiments where possible. Connecting each stage to something that pupils can observe or experience in their daily lives can also make the concept more relatable and understandable.

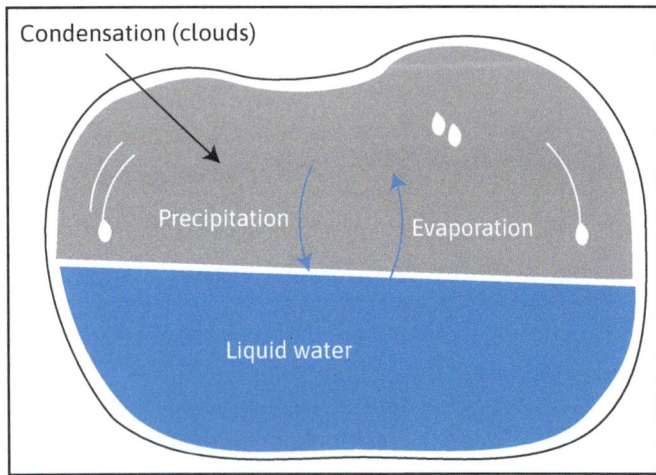

The water cycle in a polythene bag.

Key questions

○ **Can you explain what happens to a puddle of water left outside on a sunny day?**
Why does it disappear? This encourages pupils to think about the process of evaporation as a part of the water cycle.

○ **Why do you think that clouds often appear before it rains?**
This question prompts pupils to consider the role of condensation in forming clouds and leading to precipitation.

○ **What might happen to a raindrop after it falls on a garden?**
This encourages pupils to think about the various paths that water can take once it reaches the ground, such as absorption by plants, infiltration into the soil, evaporation, or run-off into rivers and eventually the ocean.

○ **Can you think of any ways that human activities might impact the water cycle?**
This pushes pupils to consider the potential effects of activities such as deforestation, urbanisation and pollution on the natural processes of the water cycle.

● Common misconceptions

○ **Water is only a liquid.**
Water exists in all three states – solid, liquid and gas. In the water cycle, water evaporates into a gas during evaporation, condenses into a liquid in the form of clouds, and can also be a solid when it precipitates as snow or hail.

○ **Evaporation only occurs when it's hot.**
While heat does speed up evaporation, it can still happen at lower temperatures. For instance, puddles evaporate and washing dries on the line even on cool days.

○ **The water that we drink is brand new.**
The water cycle includes all of the water on the Earth: the water we have on Earth today is the same water that's been around for billions of years. It's continuously cycled and recycled through the environment.

○ **All rainwater immediately runs into rivers and oceans.**
While some rainwater does flow into bodies of water, a considerable amount also seeps into the ground where it can be taken up by plant roots, or can replenish groundwater supplies. Some water also evaporates back into the atmosphere, or is transpired by plants.

● Progression

Key Stage	Development of ideas
EYFS	· Pupils are encourage to talk about the features of their own environment and how environments might vary from one to another. Basic concepts about weather, rain and where water comes from could be introduced.
KS1 (ages 5-7)	· Pupils should be taught to observe changes across the four seasons, and to describe the weather associated with the seasons. They should understand the need for water for life, and its uses. This can be used to discuss parts of the water cycle.
LKS2 (ages 7-9)	· Pupils should identify the different states of matter (solid, liquid, gas), and observe how some materials change state when they are heated or cooled. They should also describe the water cycle, including the role of the Sun in this process.
UKS2 (ages 9-11)	· Pupils should understand the processes of evaporation and condensation, and associate the rate of evaporation with temperature. They should also identify the part played by evaporation and condensation in the water cycle.
KS3 (ages 11-14)	· Pupils should understand the processes of photosynthesis and the dependence of almost all life on Earth on this process. They should also understand the interdependence of organisms in an ecosystem. This can be used to discuss the role of the water cycle in supporting life on Earth.

Rocks

The big idea of rocks is that they are a natural material, which can be used by people to make things. Rocks can naturally change over time (see **The rock cycle**).

To make the most of rocks, pupils need to know:

- what rocks can be used for: constructing buildings and bridges; making statues and sculpture; roads and paths; worktops and chopping boards, and many more;
- that there are many different types of rocks with different properties. It is useful for pupils to be able to identify, at least, limestone, slate, marble and granite; and
- that rocks are natural materials. They can be categorised into three main types based on how they were made: igneous, sedimentary and metamorphic (see **The rock cycle**).

The key problem with rocks is that they often look different in their natural state from when they have been worked. It is worth having examples of both: for example, limestone chips look different from limestone statues, and a lump of granite looks different from a polished worktop or chopping board. Show pupils examples of both worked and unworked rock to compare.

	Limestone	Marble	Slate	Granite
Unworked				
Worked				
Description	Limestone is a hard rock that is made of grains joined together. Limestone may contain fossils.	Marble is a smooth hard rock. It is often white with veins of colour.	Slate is made in thin layers. It is a grey/ black colour.	Granite is a hard rock with no layers. It is made up of crystals joined together.
Uses	Limestone is often used for buildings, bridges and pavements. It can be made into statues and sculptures. It is also important for making concrete and cement, and also iron.	Marble is used to make statues and sculptures. It can be used to make table tops and chopping boards.	Slate is used for tiles on roofs. It is also used to make snooker tables.	Granite is often used for worktops and chopping boards.

How it was formed	Limestone was made over millions of years from small pieces of shell falling to the bottom of lakes and seas. Over time, these small pieces form a hard strong rock.	Marble is made from another type of rock (limestone), which has been heated and compressed over millions of years underground.	Slate is made from another type of rock (mudstone), which has been heated and compressed over millions of years underground.	Granite is formed over millions of years as molten magma in volcanoes cools slowly and becomes solid.

Key questions

○ **How can you tell what type of rock this is?**
- If you can see crystals in the rock, it is usually an igneous rock. Granite usually has large crystals (brown sugar-sized). Basalt usually has tiny crystals – you might need a magnifying glass to see them.
- If the rock is made of grains, it is probably sedimentary, often sandstone or limestone. Chalk is a type of limestone. Fossils are most likely to be found in sedimentary rocks.
- Metamorphic rocks, such as slate or marble, are distinctive.

○ **What can you use rock for?**
Show pupils examples of rock used in everyday life, such as cladding on buildings, worktops, table tops and kitchen chopping boards.

Common misconceptions

○ **Rocks are just big stones.**
Scientists (geologists) use the word 'rock' to mean a type of rock, rather than a chunk of rock.

○ **Rocks were all made millions of years ago.**
Most rock that we see today was made millions of years ago, but new rock is still being made all the time (see **The rock cycle**).

○ **All rocks are the same.**
There are many types of rock, with different origins and chemical makeup.

○ **Concrete is a type of rock.**
Concrete is a man-made material, so it isn't considered a rock..

Progression

Key Stage	Development of ideas
EYFS & KS1 (ages 5-7)	· Pupils know that there are different types of rock and that rock can be used to build things (e.g. religious buildings, castles, bridges, pavements, etc).
KS2 (ages 7-11)	· Pupils can identify several types of rock in both worked and unworked forms (e.g. a chunk of granite and a polished piece of granite). · Pupils can link the properties of rock to its uses. · Pupils know that some rocks are made by cooling magma and others are made from small grains of rock or shell joined together.
KS3 (ages 11-14)	· Pupils are taught about the rock cycle.

Classification of rocks

The big idea about classifying rocks is understanding that all rocks on our planet, from the smallest pebble to the tallest mountain, fit into one of three categories: **igneous**, **metamorphic** and **sedimentary**. This classification hinges on the way in which these rocks are formed, and understanding it gives us a glimpse into the Earth's history, revealing the processes that have shaped our planet's surface over billions of years.

To make the most of this idea, begin by teaching your pupils how the three types of rock were formed. Igneous rocks form from cooling magma or lava, sedimentary rocks form from the accumulation and compaction of sediment, and metamorphic rocks form when existing rocks are subjected to high temperatures and pressures. Use real-world examples, such as volcanic eruptions for igneous rocks, river banks for sedimentary rocks, and mountain-building for metamorphic rocks. Visual aids can be very effective in helping pupils to grasp these concepts – consider using diagrams, pictures, or even bringing in rock samples if possible.

The key problem with teaching this concept is that the processes involved in rock formation are not immediately observable, as they take place over millions of years. This makes it difficult for pupils to fully grasp the processes just by explanation. Additionally, many rocks may look similar to the untrained eye, which can cause confusion when trying to classify them. A useful solution is to focus on the characteristics that make each rock type unique, such as the crystal structures in igneous rocks, the layering in sedimentary rocks, or the changed texture in metamorphic rocks. Incorporating interactive activities, such as a rock identification lab, could help to engage the pupils and reinforce their understanding of these differences.

Key questions

○ **Can you explain how each type of rock is formed? What are the processes involved?**

○ **How can we tell the difference between an igneous, sedimentary and metamorphic rock?**

○ **Can you give an example of each type of rock and explain why it belongs to that category?**

○ **If you found a rock outside, what clues would you look for to determine its classification?**

○ **How might the location of a rock help us to guess its classification?**

○ **Can you describe a situation where a sedimentary rock could turn into a metamorphic rock?**

Common misconceptions

○ **Pupils often confuse the word 'rock' meaning the substance, and 'a rock' meaning a lump of rock.**

○ **Concrete and other man-made materials are examples of rock.**
They are not.

○ **All rocks are dense.**
Pumice floats on water.

○ **Any crystals in rock are diamonds.**
They are much more likely to be quartz.

○ **Gemstones are not rocks.**
While some are organic in nature (e.g. amber), many gemstones are examples of polished rocks.

Progression

Key Stage	Development of ideas
EYFS	· Pupils should be encouraged to learn about the world around them. This can include simple observations of rocks and other natural materials in their environment.
KS1 (ages 5-7)	· Pupils should observe and compare a variety of natural and human-made materials, including rock. They should describe what they observe, including simple physical properties such as appearance and texture.
LKS2 (ages 7-9)	· Pupils should compare and group together different kinds of rocks on the basis of their appearance and simple physical properties. They should also learn about how fossils are formed when things that have lived are trapped within rock.
UKS2 (ages 9-11)	· Pupils' understanding of the physical world should be deepened, and this could include revisiting or expanding upon concepts introduced in LKS2.
KS3 (ages 11-14)	· Pupils should learn to relate the structure and types of rocks to the processes that formed them. This includes understanding the rock cycle and the formation of igneous, sedimentary and metamorphic rocks.

The rock cycle

The big idea of the rock cycle is that, over millions of years, rocks can change from one type to another.

To make the most of the rock cycle, pupils need to be familiar with several types of rocks. They need to know the names of the rocks (limestone, marble, granite, etc.) and whether they are sedimentary, metamorphic, or igneous.

The key problems that pupils have with the rock cycle is that you cannot see the rock cycle in action. Most of the processes take millions of years and happen deep within the Earth's crust.

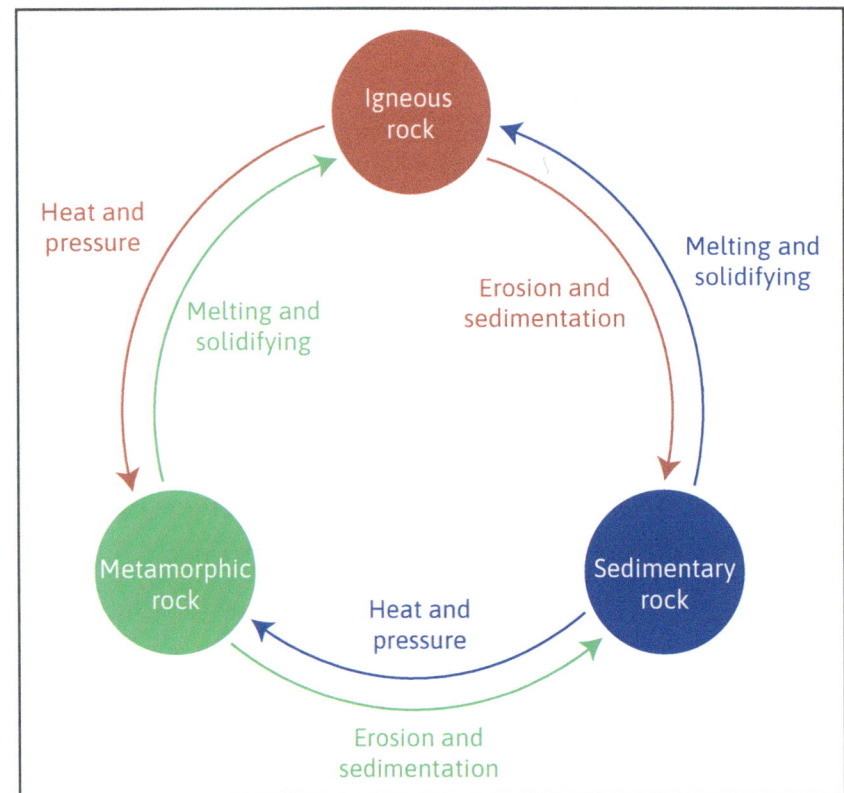

The rock cycle.

● Key questions

○ **What is the name of this type of rock?**

○ **How was this type of rock made?**

○ **How could this type of rock change into a different type?**

Common misconceptions

O **Rock never changes.**
The rock cycle describes how rocks can change over time.

O **Concrete is a type of rock.**
Concrete is a man-made material, so it isn't a type of rock.

O **Bricks are a type of rock.**
Brick is a man-made material, so it isn't a type of rock.

Progression

Key Stage	Development of ideas
EYFS	· Pupils can say whether a material is a type of rock.
KS1 (ages 5-7)	· Pupils can identify some common types of rock, including limestone, marble and granite, and state some uses.
LKS2 (ages 7-9)	· Pupils can use the rock cycle to explain how rocks can change over time.
UKS2 (ages 9-11)	· Pupils know that most fossils are found in sedimentary rocks and can explain how these are formed.
KS3 (ages 11-14)	· Pupils should understand and use the rock cycle to explain phenomena.

Erosion

The big idea about erosion is that it's a powerful force that gradually shapes our planet. Erosion is the process by which soil, rock, or other material is moved from one place to another, usually by wind, water, or ice. It's involved in creating many of the natural features that we see around us, such as valleys, coastlines and mountains. Understanding erosion can help pupils to appreciate the dynamic and ever-changing nature of Earth's landscape.

To make the most of this idea, connect erosion to familiar scenarios. This could include discussing how a local river has shaped its banks, or how a local hillside may be slowly changing over time due to erosion. Simple experiments demonstrating erosion, such as using running water to wash away a pile of dirt or sand, can also be helpful. Your aim is to take the concept from being an abstract idea to something that pupils can observe and understand.

The key challenge in teaching about erosion lies in the inherent time scales involved. Most erosion happens slowly over many years, which can make it difficult for pupils to comprehend. The idea that small, seemingly insignificant factors such as wind or flowing water can result in significant changes over time might be difficult to grasp. To overcome this, using models and time-lapse videos can help visualise this slow process in a more tangible way.

Erosion by wind and water.

● Key questions

○ **What happens to a sandcastle when a wave hits it at the beach?**
This question can help to introduce the concept of erosion by relating it to a scenario that may be familiar to the pupils.

○ **What do you think might happen to a mountain over many years of rain and wind?**
This question encourages pupils to think about the long-term effects of erosion on natural features.

○ **How do you think that plants might cause erosion?**
This question introduces the concept of how plant life can slow erosion by anchoring soil with their roots. (Note: plants can also help prevent erosion: for example, on sand dunes and river banks.)

○ **What do you think would happen to a river bank if all the plants and trees were removed?**
This question prompts pupils to apply their understanding of erosion and its relationship to plant life.

○ **Can you think of ways in which we might prevent or reduce erosion?**
This question encourages critical thinking and understanding of human interactions with the environment.

● Common misconceptions

○ **Erosion happens quickly.**
While some erosion can happen quickly, most occurs over long periods. This misconception can be reinforced by the dramatic, fast-paced erosion shown in movies or TV.

○ **All erosion is bad.**
Erosion is often associated with negative impacts, such as soil loss from farmland. However, it's also a natural process that helps to create diverse landscapes and habitats, and contributes to the formation of soil in new areas.

○ **Erosion and weathering are the same thing.**
Though they often happen together, they are different processes. Weathering involves the breaking down of rocks and minerals on the spot, while erosion involves the movement of these materials from one place to another.

● Progression

Key Stage	Development of ideas
EYFS	· Pupils should start by exploring their immediate environment, noticing changes over time, which can include basic observations of soil or sand moving.
KS1 (ages 5-7)	· Pupils could learn about the basic physical features of their environment, including how they may change over time. This can lead to an introductory discussion of erosion.
LKS2 (ages 7-9)	· Pupils should describe and understand key aspects of physical geography, which could include erosion in the context of understanding rivers and other landforms.
UKS2 (ages 9-11)	· Pupils may undertake a more in-depth study of the processes that shape landscapes, such as the effect of water and wind erosion.
KS3 (ages 11-14)	· Pupils should develop a deeper understanding of physical geography, including the processes that shape different landscapes. This can include studying erosion in detail, understanding the different types of erosion and the impacts they have on different environments.

Earthquakes

The big idea about earthquakes is that they demonstrate the dynamic nature of our Earth. They occur when there's a sudden release of energy in the Earth's crust that creates seismic waves, shaking the ground. They can be caused by natural events such as tectonic shifts, or by human activities such as mining. Understanding earthquakes is crucial, as they play a significant role in shaping the Earth's landscape and can have substantial impacts on human societies.

To make the most of this idea, try to connect the topic to situations that your pupils might recognise. For example, you could discuss earthquakes that have featured in the news, or in places that pupils might know. Modelling practical demonstrations or experiments that simulate seismic waves can also help to bring the concept to life.

The key problem in teaching about earthquakes lies in the complexity of the concepts involved. Understanding what causes earthquakes requires the grasp of ideas such as tectonic plate movement and seismic waves, which can be challenging. Explaining how seismologists measure and predict earthquakes, using concepts like magnitude and intensity, also involves some abstract thinking. Using models, diagrams and interactive tools can be very useful to help pupils visualise these complex processes.

● Key questions

○ **What causes an earthquake?**
Earthquakes are caused by the movement of the Earth's tectonic plates (large sections of the Earth's crust). When these plates move past each other, they sometimes get stuck at their edges due to friction. When the stress on the edge overcomes the friction, they suddenly move, causing an earthquake. These produce waves that travel through the Earth's crust.

○ **Why do you think that earthquakes happen more frequently in certain areas, such as the 'Ring of Fire'?**
Some areas, like the 'Ring of Fire' around the Pacific Ocean, have more earthquakes because they are located along the boundaries of tectonic plates. These are the areas where the Earth's crust is most active, leading to more frequent earthquakes and volcanic activity.

○ **How can earthquakes affect the landscape and communities?**
Earthquakes can cause a lot of damage to the landscape and communities. They can lead to landslides, change the course of rivers, or create new landforms. In populated areas, they can damage buildings and infrastructure, and pose a risk to people's safety.

○ **What are some precautions that people can take if they live in an earthquake-prone area?**
People in earthquake-prone areas can take precautions including securing heavy items in their homes to prevent them from falling, having an emergency kit ready, and practising what to do during an earthquake. Building codes in these areas often require structures to be earthquake-resistant.

○ **What might scientists monitor to predict if an earthquake is likely to occur?**
While predicting exactly when an earthquake will occur is currently beyond our technology, scientists can estimate the probability of future earthquakes based on past activity in an area. They also monitor seismic activity (small tremors that often occur before a larger earthquake), changes in groundwater levels, and unusual animal behaviour.

Common misconceptions

○ **During an earthquake, the Earth opens up.**
The Hollywood image of the ground opening up during an earthquake is largely a myth. While surface ruptures can occur, they are not the gaping chasms often depicted in movies.

○ **Big earthquakes always follow smaller ones.**
While it's true that large earthquakes are often preceded by smaller foreshocks, this is not always the case. Each earthquake is unique and cannot be predicted based on the occurrence of smaller quakes.

○ **Earthquakes are only destructive.**
Earthquakes are natural processes, which play a role in shaping the Earth's landscapes and creating geological features.

Progression

Key Stage	Development of ideas
EYFS	· Pupils are encouraged to learn and be curious about the world. This can involve a very basic introduction to the concept of the ground shaking, depending on the pupils' interests.
KS1 (ages 5-7)	· Pupils start to learn about seasonal and daily weather patterns in the UK and the location of hot and cold areas of the world. While not directly related to earthquakes, this foundation in understanding different geographical conditions can pave the way for later learning.
LKS2 (ages 7-9)	· Pupils should start to describe and understand key aspects of physical geography, which could include earthquakes in the context of understanding natural disasters or geological activity.
UKS2 (ages 9-11)	· Pupils might learn about the Earth's tectonic plates and the resulting geological activity could be introduced at this stage, providing a basis for understanding why and how earthquakes occur.
KS3 (ages 11-14)	· Pupils should deepen their understanding of geological timescales and processes, including plate tectonics, seismic activity, and how earthquakes are measured and predicted.

Fossils

The big idea about fossils is that they are the imprints or remains of plants, animals and other organisms from the remote past. They provide a record of life's long history on Earth. Fossilisation is rare, requiring specific conditions to capture a moment in biological time. Fossils offer evidence of evolution and the Earth's geologic history.

To make the most of this idea, you should first familiarise your pupils with the concept of 'deep time' (the following chapter explores this). This term is used to illustrate the immense span of geological time that Earth's history encompasses. Use analogies that pupils can relate to, such as comparing Earth's history to a calendar year, or a 24-hour clock.

The key problems in teaching about fossils are the vast time scales involved, the process of fossilisation and the interpretation of fossil records. These concepts are outside the pupils' everyday experiences.

A fossil is formed when minerals are deposited in an imprint caused by bones, shells, plants, or footprints. They take millions of years to form.

Key questions

○ **When was this living thing alive?**
Use timelines going back hundreds of millions of years to emphasise how long ago different fossils were formed. You are unlikely to be able to see on your timeline how recently humans evolved.

○ **What are fossils?**
A fossil is formed when minerals are deposited in an imprint caused by bones, shells, plants or footprints. They take millions of years to form.

○ **What can fossils tell us about the past?**
They can tell us about the shapes of living things in the past. They can also help us to understand which animals and plants existed in the same habitats.

○ **Have you seen a fossil before? Where did you see it?**

○ **Why do you think that we only have fossils of certain creatures and not others?**
Most animals and plants, when they die, don't make fossils – the conditions for making fossils are uncommon. Animals and plants that live underwater or in swampy conditions are more likely to form fossils, so we don't have as many fossils of land animals and plants.

○ **Are fossils the bones of extinct animals?**
The fossils that you can see are made of stone – they are the minerals that settled into impressions that bones made in soft mud or clay. The bone itself disappeared long ago.

Common misconceptions

○ **The fossil that I can see is made of bone.**
In actual fact, the fossil is made of minerals that have been deposited in the space left when the bones dissolve away.

○ **Only bones can be fossilised.**
Any imprint can become fossilised, including leaves, feathers and even footprints.

Progression

Key Stage	Development of ideas
EYFS	· Pupils begin to understand the concept of past and present and show curiosity about different aspects of their natural world. They engage with stories or activities that involve ancient life.
KS1 (ages 5-7)	· Pupils understand that fossils provide information about living things from long ago. · Pupils should recognise and identify common types of fossils (plants, animals). · Pupils should begin to understand the concept of extinction and its causes. · Pupils should explore different types of fossils through hands-on activities
LKS2 (ages 7-9)	· Pupils understand the process of fossilisation and how fossils are formed. · Pupils should understand that fossils are used to study Earth's history and past environments. · Pupils should learn how fossils contribute to our understanding of evolution and natural selection.
UKS2 (ages 9-11)	· Pupils understand how relative dating of fossils can indicate an organism's era. · Pupils should be able to explain how fossils provide evidence of evolution. · Pupils should be able to investigate the concept of 'living fossils'. · Pupils should understand the role of palaeontologists and how they excavate and study fossils.
KS3 (ages 11-14)	· Pupils investigate how fossil records contribute to our understanding of continental drift. · Pupils should be able to explore in depth how fossils provide evidence for evolution and extinction. · Pupils should be able to critically examine how the fossil record has gaps and its implications. · Pupils should be able to discuss ethical considerations around fossil collection and trade.

Geological deep time

The big idea about geological deep time is that Earth is incredibly old – about 4.6 billion years old. This concept helps us to understand the long history of the Earth and the slow processes that have shaped it over time, from the formation of the planet, to the movement of tectonic plates, to the evolution of life. Understanding geological deep time provides context for everything that we see around us and informs our understanding of where we might be heading.

To make the most of this idea, you should try to use timescales and models that give pupils a visual understanding of Earth's vast history. Activities could include creating timelines of Earth's history, or examining different types of fossils to understand life in different geological eras.

The key challenge in teaching about geological deep time lies in the enormity of the timescales involved. It's hard for anyone, let alone young learners, to truly grasp the concept of millions or billions of years. In addition, understanding geological deep time involves understanding many interconnected processes, such as plate tectonics, evolution and climate change. Using visual aids, models and analogies can be effective in illustrating these concepts and timescales.

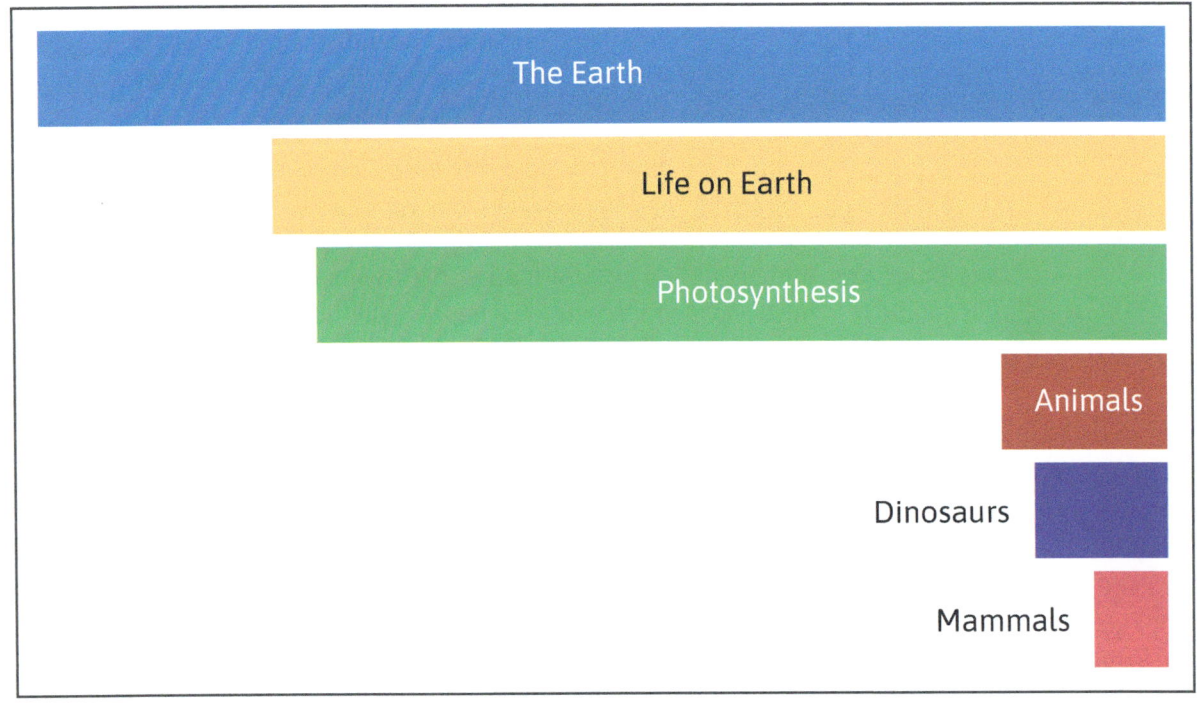

An example timeline showing geological deep time.

Key questions

- Were organism x and organism y alive at the same time?

- What happened first, x or y?

Common misconceptions

- **The Earth is not that old.**
  Given the difficulty of comprehending such large timescales, many pupils struggle to understand just how old the Earth really is.

- **Human history takes up a significant part of Earth's history.**
  In the context of geological deep time, human history is extremely short – we've been around for a mere fraction of Earth's history.

- **All fossils are the same age.**
  Fossils can be from very different times in Earth's history. The type and age of a fossil can tell us a lot about when the organism lived and what the environment was like at that time.

Progression

Key Stage	Development of ideas
EYFS	· Pupils can begin by understanding that the Earth and life on it have a past, which we can learn about by studying rocks and fossils.
KS1 (ages 5-7)	· Pupils start learning about basic geological concepts such as different types of rocks and soils. They can also learn about past life forms through the study of dinosaurs and other prehistoric creatures.
LKS2 (ages 7-9)	· Pupils can delve deeper into understanding the concept of fossils and what they tell us about the past. They can also start learning about the concept of geological time, albeit in a very simplified form.
UKS2 (ages 9-11)	· Pupils can start learning about the process of fossilisation and the major eras in Earth's history. They can also begin to understand the enormous timescales involved in geological deep time.
KS3 (ages 11-14)	· Pupils should deepen their understanding of geological deep time, exploring concepts such as evolution, plate tectonics and Earth's history in more detail. They may also learn about how we've come to understand the age of Earth and its geological history.

Volcanoes

The big idea about volcanoes is that they are openings or ruptures in the Earth's crust, through which molten rock and gas from the Earth's interior are ejected.

To make the most of this idea, you should use case studies of volcanic eruptions. These may be historic, or they may be in the news. If possible, use photos and video footage. If you or your colleagues have visited a volcano, share this experience with your pupils.

The key problem in teaching about volcanoes is that TV, movies and even classroom models can cause misconceptions. Making model volcanoes in class, using bicarbonate of soda and vinegar, can cause misconceptions about lava. Films often show volcanoes at their most active and destructive.

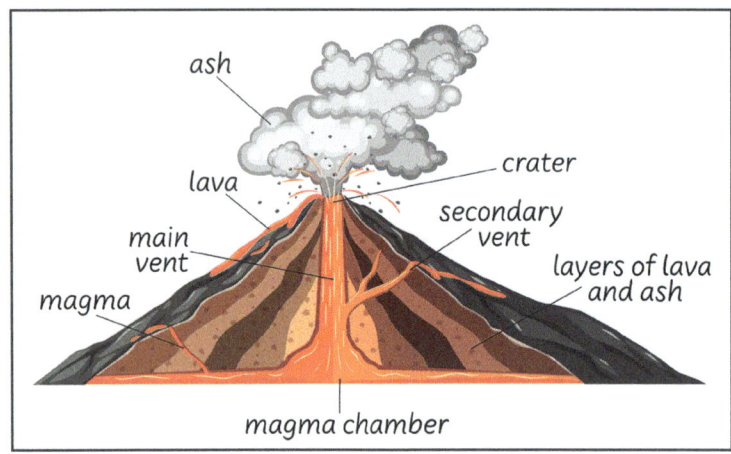

The key features of a volcano.

Key questions

○ **What causes a volcano to erupt?**
Volcanoes erupt when magma from beneath the Earth's crust rises to the surface. This can occur due to the movement of tectonic plates, or an increase in pressure below the surface.

○ **Why do you think that some volcanoes erupt violently while others erupt more gently?**
The type of eruption can be influenced by the composition of the magma. Some magma is thicker and can cause more explosive eruptions, while some is runnier and can lead to gentler, flowing eruptions.

○ **Can you think of any benefits and drawbacks of living near a volcano?**
Living near a volcano can be risky, due to the threat of eruptions that can destroy homes and be dangerous to people. However, volcanic soil is often very fertile, making it good for farming. Some regions also use geothermal energy from volcanoes for power.

○ **What might scientists monitor to predict if a volcano is about to erupt?**
Scientists can use several methods to predict volcanic eruptions. They might monitor seismic activity (earthquakes), changes in gas emissions, ground deformation (changes in the shape of the volcano), or temperature changes to try to predict when an eruption might occur.

Common misconceptions

O **All volcanoes are alike.**
Pupils often imagine one 'typical' kind of volcano – usually a cone-shaped mountain with lava spewing from the top. In reality, there are several different types of volcanoes (including shield volcanoes, cinder cones and stratovolcanoes), each with their unique structures and eruption styles.

O **Volcanoes only erupt with explosions.**
Many pupils believe that all volcanic eruptions are explosive and catastrophic, likely influenced by dramatic representations in the media. However, many volcanoes produce slow, flowing eruptions that create rivers of lava rather than explosive outbursts.

O **Volcanoes are always hot and active.**
This misconception likely stems from the images usually associated with volcanoes. In reality, many volcanoes are dormant or extinct and may not show signs of activity for thousands of years.

O **Lava is the only thing that comes out of a volcano.**
While lava is a significant part of many eruptions, volcanoes also emit gases and ash. Pyroclastic flows (a high-density mix of hot lava blocks, pumice, ash and volcanic gas) are particularly dangerous.

O **Volcanoes are only destructive.**
While it's true that volcanoes can cause damage, they also play a crucial role in building and shaping landscapes, creating new land and providing rich soil.

Progression

Key Stage	Development of ideas
EYFS	· Pupils should be encouraged to develop a sense of curiosity about the world. This can include simple discussions about natural features in their environment, which might extend to a basic introduction to volcanoes if this arises from the pupils' interests.
KS1 (ages 5-7)	· Pupils should be taught about basic physical geographical features, including hills, mountains and rivers. They should start learning about seasonal and daily weather patterns in the UK and the location of hot and cold areas of the world.
LKS2 (ages 7-9)	· Pupils should describe and understand key aspects of physical geography, including climate zones, biomes and vegetation belts, rivers, mountains, volcanoes and earthquakes, and the water cycle.
UKS2 (ages 9-11)	· Pupils might delve more into the processes that lead to volcanic formations. This includes learning about the Earth's tectonic plates, how they move, and the resulting geological activity.
KS3 (ages 11-14)	· Pupils should expand their understanding of physical geography relating to geological timescales and processes. This can include more in-depth study of volcanoes, understanding the different types of volcanoes, how they form, and the impact that they have on the surrounding environment.

How to weigh things

The big idea of weighing things in science is that it helps pupils to develop an understanding of the amount of a substance (its mass) and accurate measurement.

To make the most of weighing things pupils need to be taught:

- how to use a variety of balances and scales (Note: in science, we generally call any device that measures mass a 'balance');
- how to 'zero' the balance so that it shows zero when there is none of the substance you want to measure; and
- how to calculate the change in mass.

The key problems that pupils have with balances include:

- that there are different types of balances, which require different skills to use;
- that pupils often don't set the balance to zero before measuring; and
- that pupils often weigh the container as well as the substance that they want to measure.

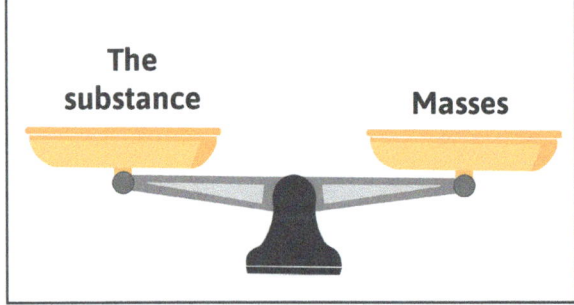

A simple balance.

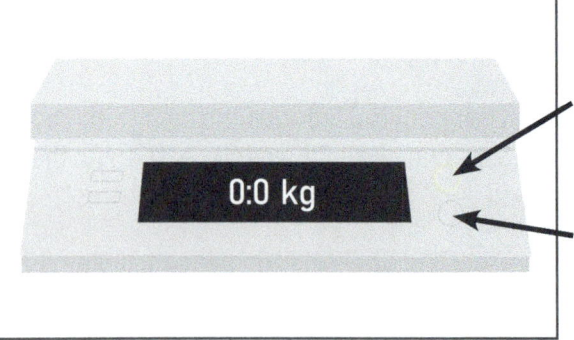

Units button (often grams and ounces).

Zero button (often labelled 'tare')

An electronic balanace.

The common features of balances.

Key questions

○ **How will you measure how much of this substance there is?**
Pupils might measure the volume of the substance (see **Measuring volume**), or the mass.

○ **Does it matter how much substance you use?**

○ **How do you set the balance to zero?**

Common misconceptions

○ **Pupils often forget to set the balance to zero.**

○ **Pupils often set the balance to measure the wrong units (you typically want grams).**

○ **Pupils often confuse 'mass' and 'weight'.**
Mass is the amount of substance (usually measured in grams and kilograms), whereas weight tells you the force of gravity acting on it (usually measures in newtons). We usually want to measure 'mass' with a balance.

Progression

Key Stage	Development of ideas
EYFS	· Pupils should experience basic concepts of weight and mass, such as heavy and light, through hands-on activities. They could use simple balance scales to compare the weight of different objects.
KS1 (ages 5-7)	· Pupils should begin to measure and compare mass/weight using appropriate vocabulary (heavier, lighter, etc.). They might use balance scales, possibly including non-standard units of measurement, to compare the weights/masses of different objects.
LKS2 (ages 7-9)	· Pupils should be introduced to standard units of measurement for mass (such as grams and kilograms) and use balances to measure accurately. They should start to use their understanding of mass in mathematical and scientific contexts. · Pupils can begin to distinguish between mass (the amount of substance) and weight (the force acting on the substance).
UKS2 (ages 9-11)	· Pupils should continue to develop their skills in weighing and measuring, including solving problems involving mass and using balances with increased accuracy. They can also develop the relationship between mass and weight.
KS3 (ages 11-14)	· Pupils should be able to use balances with precision in scientific experiments. This might include understanding the principle of moments and using a balance to calculate forces. They should also be able to analyse and present data involving measurements of weight/mass.

How to use a thermometer

The big idea of thermometers is that they measure the temperature of a substance. There are two main types of thermometer (pupils should learn how to use both): digital thermometers and liquid-in-glass thermometers.

To make the most of thermometers, pupils need to know two key points:

- thermometers don't measure the temperature instantly: it takes a short time (typically 10-30 seconds) to reach the correct temperature; and
- never take the thermometer out of the substance while you are measuring the temperature (otherwise you are measuring the temperature of the air).

Often pupils need to measure temperature repeatedly at fixed time intervals (e.g. measure the temperature of cooling water every minute for 10 minutes). Pupils should leave the thermometer in the substance for the full time of the practical.

The key problems that pupils have with thermometers include:

- that different liquid-in-glass thermometers have different scales (which can make them tricky to read);
- that digital thermometers often give readings to decimal places, which younger pupils may find hard to read;
- that all thermometers take time to adjust to the correct temperature. Either leave the thermometer in place throughout the experiment, or give it time to adjust before reading the temperature; and
- that glass thermometers are fragile. Keep them away from the edges of tables (they roll off), and don't use them to stir – they may break.

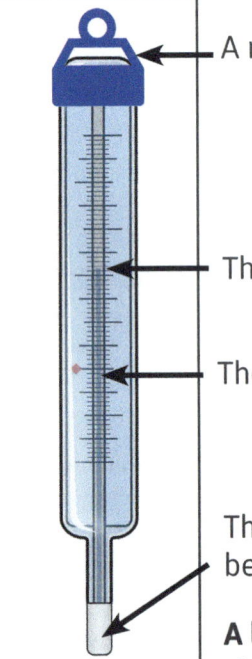

A rubber cap to stop the thermometer rolling off the table.

The reading: where the thread stops.

The thread: the liquid in the tube.

The bulb: this is the part which measures the temperature – it must be in contact with what you are measuring

A liquid-in-glass thermometer with an anti-roll cap. The scale is the simplest to read, with one division per °C.

● Key questions

○ **What is the thermometer measuring?**
Thermometers measure temperature, not heat.

○ **What end of the thermometer is measuring the temperature?**
The thermometer measures the temperature at the bulb. You must put the bulb into or next to whatever you are measuring.

○ **Where should your thermometer be between measurements?**
If you are making several temperature measurements over time, it is best to keep the thermometer in place (e.g. in the mug of hot water). When you do take it out, make sure that the thermometer is not put down where it can fall off the table and smash.

● Common misconceptions

○ **Pupils often remove the thermometer to read the temperature.**
Keep it in contact throughout the measurement.

○ **Pupils often don't leave the thermometer in the substance they are measuring long enough for the thermometer to show the correct reading.**
It usually takes at least 30 seconds to adjust to the correct temperature.

○ **Pupils leave the thermometer on the side of a table where it can fall off.**

○ **Pupils often think that some materials are naturally warmer or colder than others.**
For example, they may think that a polystyrene cup is warmer than a china cup because of how it feels to the touch. This confusion arises because insulating materials prevent heat leaving your skin quickly, whereas conducting materials feel cold to the touch even if the temperature is the same.

● Progression

Key Stage	Development of ideas
EYFS & KS1 (ages 5-7)	· Pupils should be able to use language such as 'warmer than' and 'colder than' and rank objects by temperature (e.g. wooden blocks, or water from the fridge, shady spot, radiator, etc.) through touch.
LKS2 (ages 7-9)	· Pupils could start with digital thermometers to measure the temperature of different objects (check that they can interpret the decimal place before using).
UKS2 (ages 9-11)	· Pupils should be able to use liquid-in-glass thermometers to measure the temperature of different objects. They should take readings at fixed intervals (e.g. a cooling cup of tea). **Don't take the thermometer out of the liquid to measure the temperature.**
KS3 (ages 11-14)	· Pupils should choose the most appropriate thermometer for the purpose. They may use dataloggers to measure temperature.

Measuring time

The big idea about measuring time is that this allows us to accurately measure how quickly or slowly a process takes place. Accurate time measurement is crucial in many areas, from cooking, to sports, to scientific experiments.

To make the most of this idea, you should ensure that pupils understand how a stopwatch functions. This includes the basics of starting, stopping and resetting the timer, as well as calculating the elapsed time. Pupils need practical, hands-on experience.

The key problem in teaching how to measure time accurately using a stopwatch is that it can be easy for pupils to make mistakes when operating the device, such as failing to press the start or stop button at the correct time, or struggling to read the elapsed time accurately, especially when they are concentrating on other elements in the experiment. This can be particularly challenging when dealing with very short time intervals. To mitigate these issues, it's beneficial to practise using the stopwatch in different scenarios, as well as focusing on how to accurately read and record the time displayed. It's also important to discuss potential sources of error and how they can be reduced, reinforcing the importance of precision when measuring time.

A typical stopwatch.
Try to use stopwatches or stopclocks with the simplest displays (some have hours:minutes :seconds:milliseconds, which pupils can find confusing). Also, take care over the buttons (often labelled lap, reset and start/stop) – they can be confusing and frustrating. Specialist school stopclocks are often worth the expense.

Materials needed:
- Stopwatch (or a clock with a second hand)
- An event to measure (e.g. how long it takes for a parachute to fall, a truck to roll down a slope, or a snail to find a lettuce leaf).

Step-by-step method:
- **Introduction and demonstration:** Explain to the pupils what they will be doing. Demonstrate how the stopwatch or clock works, making sure to explain the minute, second and (if present) millisecond hands or displays.
- **Prepare and practise timing:** timing requires pupils to pay attention to the clock and the event at the same time: consider practising using the stopwatch separately. Working in pairs can reduce the cognitive load if practised beforehand.

- **Start the event and timer simultaneously:** When the event begins, start the stopwatch or note the time on the clock. If you're using a clock, make sure that the second hand is at the 12 o'clock position for easy reading. Working in pairs often makes this easier: the partner managing the event can do a countdown for the timing partner.
- **Stop the timer:** As soon as the event finishes, stop the stopwatch or note the time on the clock again. Calculate the elapsed time if using a clock.
- **Record the time:** Write down the time that it took for the event to occur. You could use a whiteboard, or large piece of paper, where everyone can see it. For older primary pupils, you could also introduce the concept of a data table to record each measurement.
- **Repeat the event for accuracy:** Encourage pupils to repeat the event several times and record the time each time. This repetition not only gives them practice in measuring time, but also demonstrates the concept of variability in measurements.
- **Calculate average time:** Discuss with pupils whether any of the results are the result of errors in the event or in the timing, and remove them. Then calculate the average of the remaining times. For younger pupils, you can demonstrate this process, while older pupils may be able to help with the calculations.

Useful terms

- **Accuracy** refers to how close a measurement is to the true value. For example, if you use a stopclock to time a 100-meter sprint, and the true time taken by the athlete is exactly 10.00 seconds, an accurate stopwatch reading would be one that is very close to this true time, such as 10.01 seconds or 9.99 seconds.
- **Precision** relates to the fineness of the measurement or the smallest increment that can be measured. For a stopwatch, the precision is not necessarily the smallest increment shown on the stopwatch: human reaction time limits the precision to about half a second.
- **Reliability** involves the consistency of a set of measurements or the repeatability of the measurements. If every time you use the stopwatch to measure the 100-meter sprint under the same conditions, you get very similar results, then the timing is reliable. Reliable measurements can be consistently repeated.

● Key questions

○ **How precise can you be with a stopwatch?**
If a person is timing, the best possible precision is about 0.5 seconds. However, a data logging timer can be much more precise.

○ **How do you know if your result is reliable?**
Repeat the timing several times and see how close the readings are.

● Progression

Key Stage	Development of ideas
EYFS	· Pupils should begin to understand the concept of time in a very basic way, such as morning, afternoon and night. Simple experiments related to day and night, seasons and other naturally-occurring phenomena can help them to understand the passage of time. Teachers can also introduce simple tools such as an hourglass or a basic clock to help them to visualise time passing.
KS1 (ages 5-7)	· Pupils can be taught about seconds, minutes and hours. Simple experiments measuring time using a stopwatch can be useful. For example, time how long it takes an ice cube to melt, or a seed to sprout.
LKS2 (ages 7-9)	· Pupils should be able to use digital and analog clocks to tell the time. They can be involved in more complex experiments in which time measurement is required, for example, tracking the growth of a plant over weeks, observing the phases of the Moon, or studying the rate of a chemical reaction.
UKS2 (ages 9-11)	· Pupils can engage in more long-term investigations, requiring them to measure and record time over extended periods (days, weeks, or even months). They can also start to learn about data representation, graphing time on the x-axis of a graph to show changes over time, and use software tools for data visualisation and analysis.
KS3 (ages 11-14)	· Pupils can start to understand more complex concepts including speed (distance/time) and rate (change/time). They can do experiments such as calculating the speed of a rolling ball, the rate of evaporation of water, or the rate of growth of a plant. They can calculate the average speed, velocity and acceleration in physics experiments. In chemistry, they can learn about reaction rates. At this stage, pupils should be capable of using sophisticated measurement tools, and collecting and interpreting data.

How to use a microscope

The big idea of using a microscope in the primary science classroom is that it reveals a whole new microscopic world to the eyes of the pupils.

To make the most of a microscope in the classroom, there are several things to consider:
- Do you know how to use the microscope yourself?
- Can you focus and adjust the magnification?
- Can you make a microscope slide?

Practise these things so that you can both explain and demonstrate to pupils and also support quickly and efficiently when your pupils struggle.

Many microscopes can project onto screens in the classroom – this is a very powerful feature. If you only have one or two microscopes, set them up at the front where you can supervise and get pupils up in small groups to use them while the others are busy on a task.

Materials needed:
- Microscope
- Microscope slides
- Cover slips
- Specimen (what you want to look at)
- Dropper or tweezers
- Blank paper and coloured pencils (for sketching what you see)

Step-by-step method:
- Placement: Place the microscope on a flat surface where it won't be disturbed.
- Setting up: Plug the microscope into a power source if it needs one. Make sure that it's turned off before you start.
- Understanding parts: Familiarise yourself with the parts of the microscope. The eyepiece is where you look through. The objectives are the different lenses that you can rotate to zoom in or out. The stage is where you place your specimen. The light source is underneath the stage.
- Prepare your specimen: If you're looking at something solid, such as a leaf or bug wing, carefully place it on the slide. If you're looking at something liquid, like pondwater, use a dropper to put a small drop on the slide. Carefully put the cover slip on top of the specimen to protect it.
- Placing the slide: Place the slide on the stage and secure it with the stage clips.
- Light source: Turn on the light source.
- Start with lowest magnification: Rotate the objectives to the lowest magnification lens (usually 4x or 10x).
- Focus: Look through the eyepiece and turn the coarse focus knob until the image starts to come into focus. Fine tune the image by slowly turning the fine focus knob.

- Increasing magnification: If you want to see the specimen more closely, carefully rotate to the next highest magnification. You'll need to use the focus knobs again each time that you change magnification.
- Sketching: Draw what you see on a piece of paper. Label the parts that you recognise.
- Safety: When you've finished, turn off the light, remove the slide and cover the microscope to keep it clean.

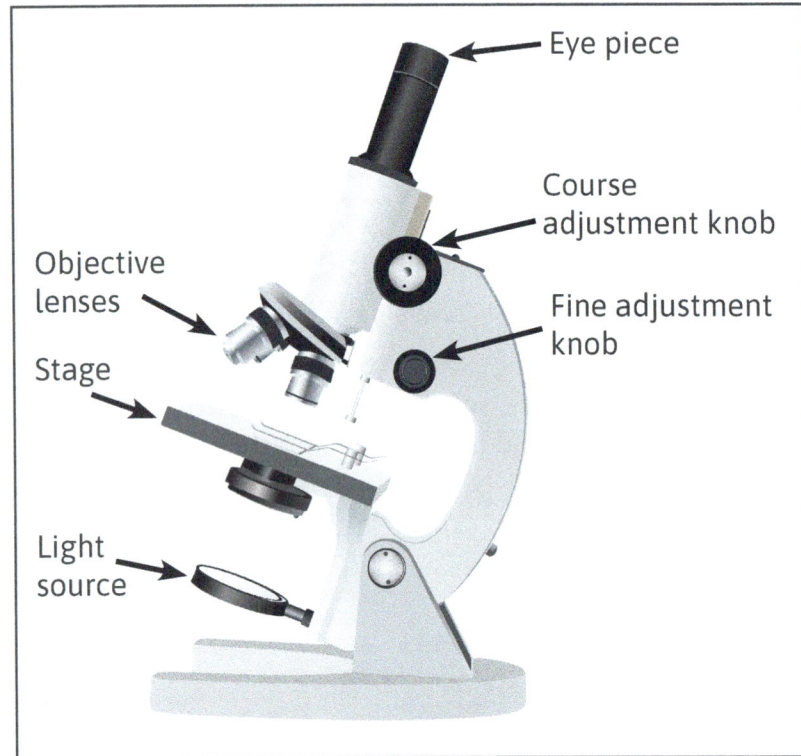

Eye piece

Course adjustment knob

Objective lenses

Fine adjustment knob

Stage

Light source

A traditional class microscope.

Examples of when you might use a microscope in Key Stage 2 (ages 7-11) science:

- *Living Things and Their Habitats*: Investigate the small creatures that live in different habitats. You could take a sample of pondwater and look at the microscopic organisms living in it.
- *Plants*: Look at the structure of leaves, or the roots of a plant. You might be able to see the tiny holes (stomata) on a leaf where it 'breathes'.
- *Animals, Including Humans*: Examine a strand of hair, or a drop of saliva, to see what human cells look like.
- *Materials and Their Properties*: Compare the structure of different materials. For example, you could look at a piece of fabric, a paper towel and a plastic bag to see how their structures differ.

Remember, always handle the microscope and specimens with care, and ask an adult for help if needed. Happy exploring!

Key questions

What do you think we might see with a microscope that we can't see with our naked eyes?
We can the detailed structures of small objects like leaves or insect parts that are too small to be seen without magnification.

Why is it important to handle the microscope carefully?
Microscopes are delicate and expensive instruments. Handling them carefully ensures that they remain in good condition and provide accurate observations.

Why might we want to change the magnification of the microscope?
Changing the magnification will make the objects appear larger and reveal more details, but it will also reduce the area that we can see at one time.

How do you think scientists use microscopes in their work?
Can you give any examples? Scientists use microscopes to study cells, bacteria and viruses to understand diseases, to examine the structure of materials in fields like materials science, and to observe environmental samples in ecology, among other uses.

Progression

Key Stage	Development of ideas
KS1 (ages 5-7)	· Pupils should be able to use magnifying glasses.
LKS2 (ages 7-9)	· Pupils should be able to use magnifying glasses and simple digital microscopes.
UKS2 (ages 9-11)	· Pupils should be able to use simple microscopes and simple digital microscopes.
KS3 (ages 11-14)	· Pupils should be able to use simple microscopes and simple digital microscopes.

How to measure the volume of liquids

The big idea of measuring the volumes of liquids is that volume is a key measurement in science as well as in everyday life – especially in the kitchen.

To make the most of measuring volume, pupils need to measure volumes many times in different contexts.

One key problem that pupils have with measuring volume is that we use so many different units, including pints, gallons, litres, centimetres cubed, millilitres, cups, tablespoons and teaspoons.

Another key problem is that pupils are often confused by a container's shape: a tall thin litre container holds the same amount of liquid as a shorter, wider container.

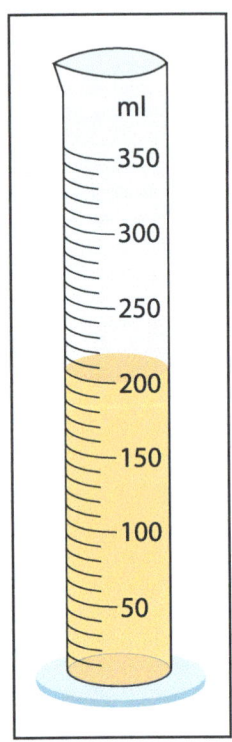

This curved surface is called the meniscus. For accurate measurement, you should measure the flat part of the meniscus.

200

150

To read the scale accurately, put your eye at the same level as the flat part of the meniscus.

● Key questions

○ **Which container holds the most liquid?**
Give pupils the experience of comparing different size and shape containers.

○ **What might you use this measuring container to measure?**
Give pupils practical examples of measuring volumes, e.g. teaspoons of sugar and salt, cups of tea and coffee, pints and litres of milk, millilitres of water or sunflower oil.

● Common misconceptions

○ **All containers of the same height hold the same volume.**
Many pupils might think that the taller the container, the more liquid it can hold. They may not initially consider the width or shape of the container as factors. Show them differently-sized and shaped containers that all hold the same volume to dispel this misconception.

○ **The position of the meniscus doesn't matter.**
When reading a measurement from a graduated cylinder or a measuring jug, it's important to read from the flat part of the meniscus. Some pupils might not understand this and could read the measurement from the top of the meniscus instead.

○ **All liquids have the same density.**
Some pupils might assume that one litre of water has the same mass as one litre of another liquid, such as oil or honey. Introduce them to the concept of density by showing that different liquids can have different weights, even if their volumes are the same (e.g. use a number of identical containers. Fill each with a different liquid, including water. Put each on a balance to see which is heaviest. The key learning is that some liquids are more dense than others.)

○ **Measuring volume is always exact.**
While measuring tools can provide a close estimation, several factors can cause minor inaccuracies, such as the precision of the jug or cylinder, the temperature of the liquid, and human error. This could be an opportunity to introduce the idea of significant figures and measurement error.

● Progression

Key Stage	Development of ideas
EYFS	· Pupils should start by exploring different quantities and sizes in a practical, hands-on way. They might play with water in a sand and water table, for example, pouring it from one container to another and seeing which is fuller.
KS1 (ages 5-7)	· Pupils should be able to compare, describe and solve practical problems for capacities and volumes (for example, full/empty, more than, less than, half, half-full, quarter). They should also begin to measure and record capacity and volume using graduated jugs or simple measuring cylinders
LKS2 (ages 7-9)	· Pupils should continue to measure, compare, add and subtract volumes/capacities. They should use the appropriate units, convert between units (litres to millilitres), and learn to read scales with increasing precision.
UKS2 (ages 9-11)	· Pupils should use their knowledge to solve problems involving converting between units of time. They should also estimate volume (using litres/millilitres) and capacity.
KS3 (ages 11-14)	· Pupils will use this understanding in various scientific experiments that require accurate measurement of different liquids. They should understand the importance of precision and accuracy in scientific measurements and investigations.

How to use forcemeters

The big idea is how to use a forcemeter (or Newtonmeter) to measure forces accurately and precisely.

To make the most of forcemeters in your science lessons, you need to be able to:
- choose one with an appropriate scale;
- set the forcemeter to zero; and
- read the scale accurately.

The key problems with forcemeters happen when you use one with the wrong scale, or forget to 'zero' the forcemeter (so that it reads zero when no force is applied).

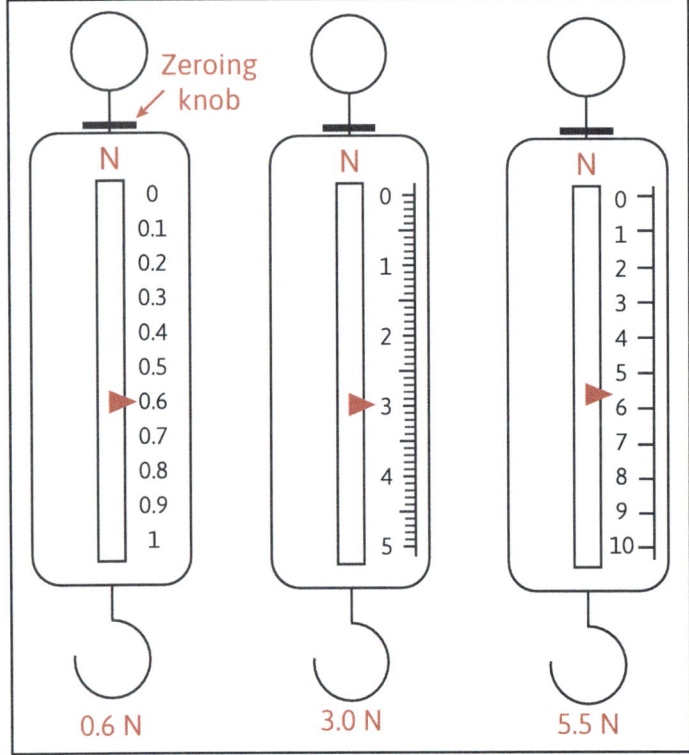

0.6 N   3.0 N   5.5 N

Three different scales commonly used on forcemeters. Either only give out identical forcemeters, or train your pupils to read the various scales.

● Key questions

○ **How do you choose a forcemeter with the correct scale?**
Test the forcemeter with the largest force that you will need to measure in the experiment. The needle on your forcemeter should move at least half-way along the scale, but not reach the end of the scale. If not, find a forcemeter with a more appropriate scale.

○ **How do you 'zero' the forcemeter?**
Make sure that it shows zero when no force is applied. At one end of the forcemeter, you will find an adjusting knob. Turn the knob with the forcemeter unloaded until the pointer reads zero.

○ **How do you read the scale accurately?**
You can often measure with one more digit of precision than the numbers on the scale. For example, you may only have whole numbers on the scale, but be able to measure accurately to one decimal place (see the diagram above).

Common mistakes and misconceptions

○ **Common mistakes include:**
- failing to set zero before you begin;
- reading the scale incorrectly;
- choosing a forcemeter with an inappropriate scale (if the forcemeter can measure very big forces, the needle will barely move; if it can read very small forces, the needle is likely to reach the end of the scale); and
- Even though scales measure weight (relying on the Earth's gravity to act on the mass of the object), the units are often in grams and kilograms – units of mass. If a set of scales made for the Earth were taken to the Moon, the lower gravity would mean that a 50 kg person would only appear to have a mass of 8.5 kg (even though their mass would actually still be 50 kg).

Progression

Key Stage	Development of ideas
EYFS	· Pupils should be able to talk about the forces that they experience (pushes, pulls and twists). Pupils should say whether forces are large or small.
KS1 (ages 5-7)	· Pupils identify forces in different contexts and talk about them. They will be able to talk about pushes, pulls and twists and apply these words to everyday situations, such as in the playground. Pupils will be able to compare approximate sizes of forces.
LKS2 (ages 7-9)	· Pupils expand their concept of forces and their sizes. They will use sentences such as: 'The closer the magnets, the stronger the force' and 'The bigger the force, the more the material stretches'. Pupils may begin to use forcemeters to measure weight and friction.
UKS2 (ages 9-11)	· Pupils should be skilled at zeroing forcemeters, reading scales and using a forcemeter in a variety of contexts, including measuring friction, weight, tension and buoyancy, and air resistance. · Pupils should understnd that forces can be multipled or reduced and apply this to levers, gears and pulleys. Competence with forcemeters allows pupils to experience this effect quantitatively.
KS3 (ages 11-14)	· Pupils should be familiar with forcemeters to support their understanding of balanced and unbalanced forces, moment as the turning effect of a force, and forces associated with deforming objects. · Pupils should know that Hooke's law explains how most forcemeters work.

How to manage lessons with circuits

The big idea is that circuit lessons are difficult to manage. Circuits are prone to going wrong, and it is common for many groups of pupils to need support at the same time.

To make the most of circuits, you need to be prepared. You can make the lesson more successful by checking the components and planning how you will give them out. In the lesson, you will need to troubleshoot any faulty circuits efficiently.

The key challenge with using circuits in your lesson is logistical: how can you help each pupil to fix their circuit quickly and efficiently when other pupils are waiting for help?

- Before the lesson, you should test each component that your class will need. Cells may go flat stored in a tray, bulbs may have been returned broken, and wires often stop conducting because of breaks in their plugs, or in the wires under the insulation. Test and remove each faulty component and either fix it or get rid of it. The best way to do this is to:
  - set up a circuit that works;
  - remove one wire from your working circuit and replace it with each wire in turn. Remove any faulty wires; and
  - repeat for each component in the faulty circuit.

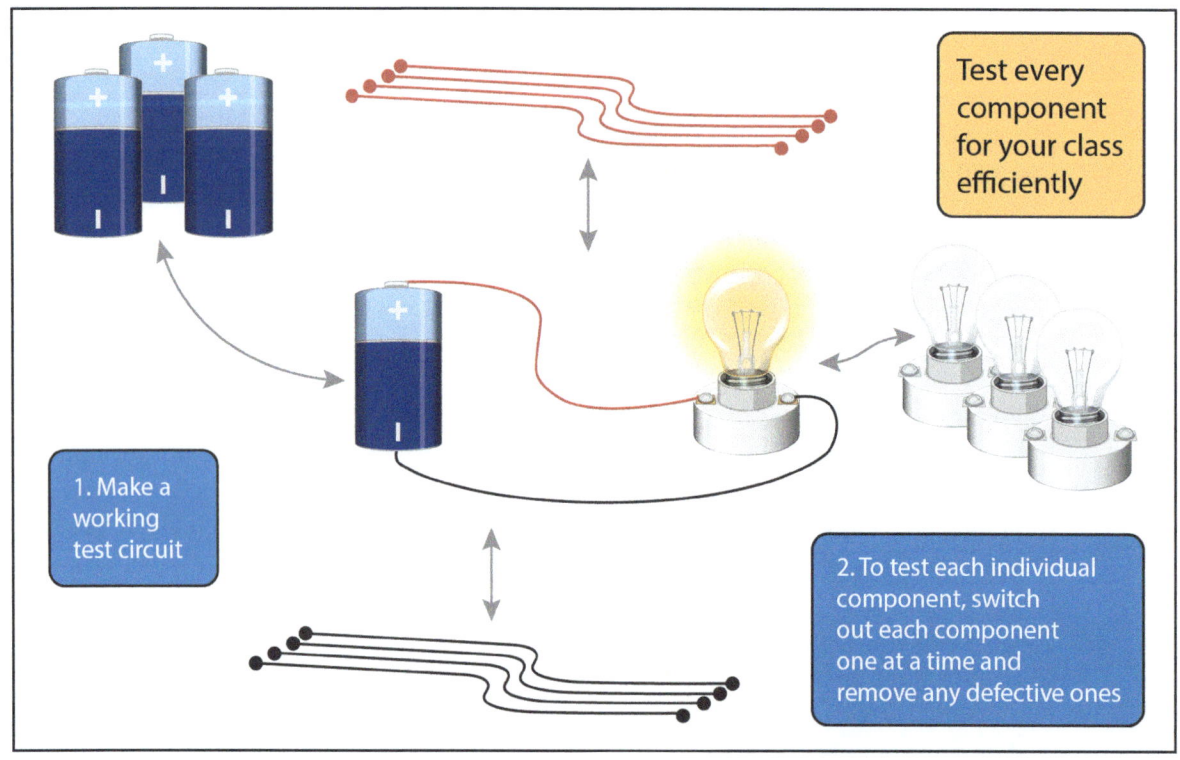

Test every component for your class efficiently

1. Make a working test circuit

2. To test each individual component, switch out each component one at a time and remove any defective ones

- Model how to make the circuit. Visualisers are great for this.
- Distribute the wires, bulbs and cells efficiently:

Distribution method #1	Distribution method #2
Give each group a tray containing the components that they need.	1. Ask one member of each group to collect one bulb and return to their table. 2. Then ask another member of each group to collect one cell and return to their table. 3. Finally, ask another member of each group to collect the correct number of wires.

- Put a working circuit in your class in a convenient place so that pupils can test their components if their circuits don't work. Train pupils to follow the process of testing their components one by one. Train any other adults in the room to support.

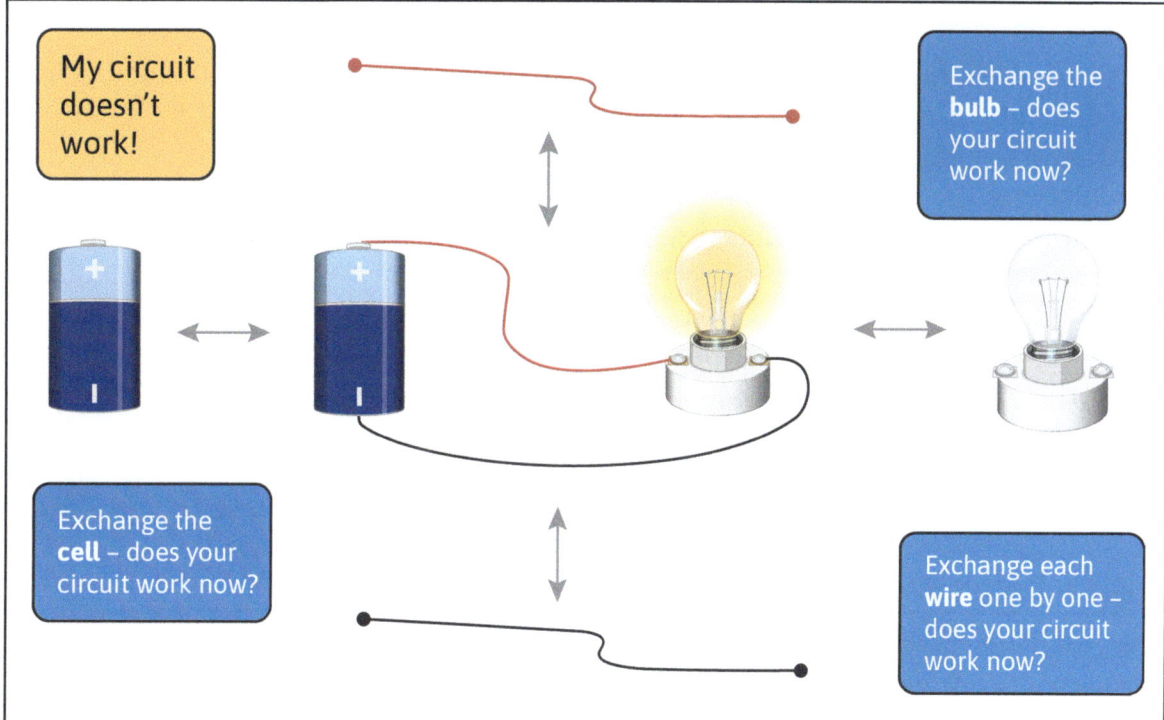

- Have a tray for faulty components in the class and train pupils to use it.
- Tidying away: After the lesson, detangle the wires. Repair any faulty components that you can. Dispose of anything that you can't repair. Never put a faulty component away.

Representing data

The big idea about representing data in charts is that visual representations of data make the data easier to analyse and evaluate. Typically, we use pictograms, bar graphs, pie charts and line graphs.

To make the most of this idea, pupils should practise drawing and interpreting different types of chart. It is also important that pupils understand the characteristics of different types of chart and when to use them. Each chart type is suited to different data sets and situations, and being able to choose the right one is crucial for effective data representation.

The key problem in teaching the representation of data in charts is that pupils need to understand what types of data they are using:

- Continuous numbers – the numbers can have any values, including decimals. For example, a person's height or mass can have any value.
- Discrete numbers – the numbers can only have certain values (typically whole numbers), for example the number of items.
- Categoric values – these values are the categories that we are measuring. For example, if we were counting minibeasts, we could count the following categories: woodlice, spiders and insects.

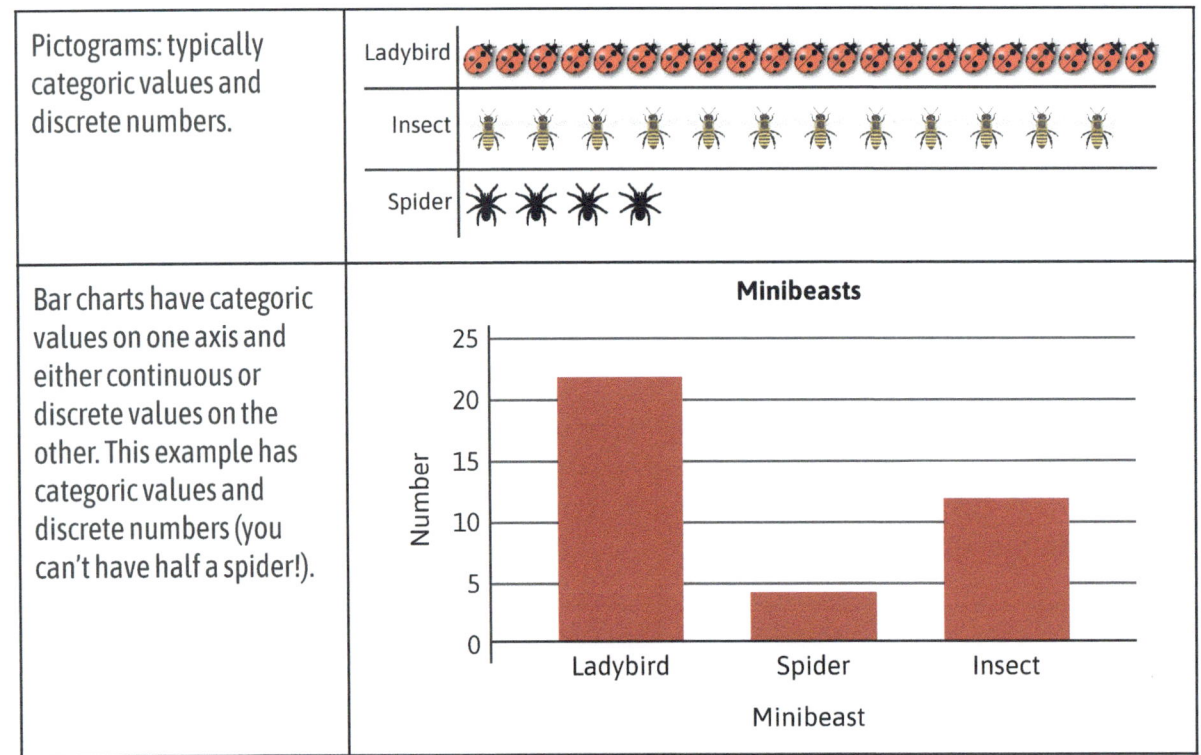

Pictograms: typically categoric values and discrete numbers.	
Bar charts have categoric values on one axis and either continuous or discrete values on the other. This example has categoric values and discrete numbers (you can't have half a spider!).	

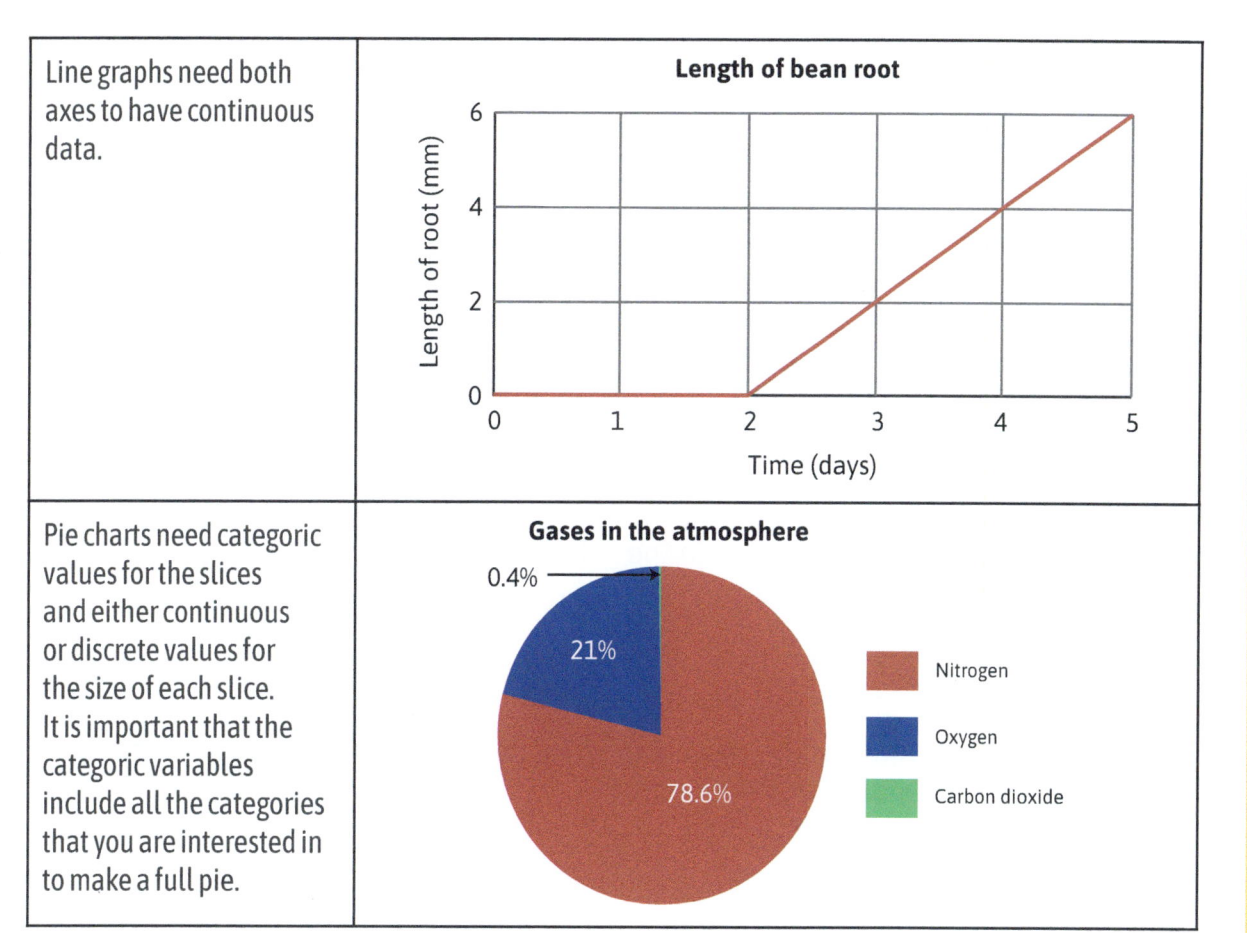

| Line graphs need both axes to have continuous data. | **Length of bean root** |
| Pie charts need categoric values for the slices and either continuous or discrete values for the size of each slice. It is important that the categoric variables include all the categories that you are interested in to make a full pie. | **Gases in the atmosphere** |

Key questions

O **Are you comparing values?**
Bar graphs and pie charts are good for comparing quantities. A bar graph is useful for comparing quantities across categories, while a pie chart is good for showing the proportion of the whole that each category represents.

O **Are you showing how something changes over time?**
If the pupils' data involve a time, a line graph may be the most effective choice.

O **Are you trying to show parts of a whole?**
Pie charts are typically used when the pupil wants to show how individual parts contribute to a whole.

Common mistakes and misconceptions

Pictograms:

O **Equal representation:** Pupils often assume that each picture or icon in a pictogram represents one unit, while it can represent any number of units (2, 5, 10, etc.). It's important to check the key to understand what each picture represents.

O **Part of a picture:** When a picture or icon is divided, pupils might disregard the fact that each part also represents a specific number of units.

Bar charts:

- ○ **Scaling:** Pupils often misinterpret the scale, especially when it's not incremented by ones. This can lead to inaccurate reading of the graph.

- ○ **Width of bars:** The width of the bars in a bar chart has no meaning and all bars should have the same width. Some pupils might think that wider bars represent a greater value.

- ○ **Starting point:** Bar charts should always start at zero on the y-axis. Pupils often forget this when drawing their own bar charts, which can lead to misinterpretation of the data.

Line graphs:

- ○ **Individual points:** Line graphs represent a trend over time, or another continuous variable. Some pupils may focus on individual points and not understand the overall trend that the graph is showing.

- ○ **Flat lines:** Pupils may incorrectly interpret flat lines as showing no data or missing data, rather than representing no change in the value of the dependent variable.

Pie charts:

- ○ **Comparing slices:** It can be hard to accurately compare the sizes of different slices, especially if they are similar in size. Pupils often misjudge which slice is bigger and by how much.

- ○ **Understanding percentages:** Pie charts often use percentages to represent each category's contribution to the whole. Pupils may struggle with understanding how these percentages translate into parts of a whole.

- ○ **Order of slices:** The order of slices in a pie chart is arbitrary, but pupils might interpret the order as meaningful.

Progression

Key Stage	Development of ideas
KS1 (ages 5-7)	· Pupils should be able to understand simple pictograms, tally charts, block diagrams and tables. · Pupils should be able to ask and answer questions about totalling and comparing categorical data.
KS2 (ages 7-11)	· Pupils should be able to interpret and present data using bar charts, pictograms and tables. · Pupils should be able to solve one-step and two-step questions using information presented in bar charts and pictograms and tables. · Pupils should be able to interpret and present discrete and continuous data using appropriate graphical methods, including bar charts and time graphs. · Pupils should be able to solve comparison, sum and difference problems using information presented in bar charts, pictograms, tables and other graphs.
KS3 (ages 11-14)	· Pupils should be able to interpret and construct pie charts and line graphs and use these to solve problems. · Pupils should be able to calculate and interpret the mean as an average. · Pupils should be able to complete, read and interpret information in tables, charts and graphs. · Pupils should be able to associate a frequency distribution or a cumulative frequency distribution with its graphical representation. · Pupils should be able to describe, interpret and compare observed distributions of a single variable through: appropriate graphical representation involving discrete, continuous and grouped data; and appropriate measures of central tendency (mean, mode, median) and spread (range, consideration of outliers).

How to manage a science cupboard

The big idea of a science cupboard is to make science teaching using practical equipment simple to prepare. Here are some instructions on how to manage a primary school science resources cupboard effectively:

- **Inventory:** Start by creating a complete inventory of all science equipment in the cupboard. Categorise the items based on the type of experiments that they are used for, or the area of science they belong to, for instance, chemistry, physics, biology, geology, etc.

- **Organise:** Next, organise the items according to their categories. Use shelves, boxes, or bins for different categories. Label everything clearly. Small items can be stored in clear, plastic containers, so that their contents are visible. Larger items can be placed on shelves.

- **Label:** Create a labelling system for all the items. The labels should be clear and easy to read. You might want to consider colour-coding for different categories. The labelling should include the name of the item, the quantity, and the category to which it belongs.

- **Map:** Create a map or diagram of the cupboard, showing where each category of items is stored. Post this on the inside of the cupboard door, or somewhere easily visible, so that all teachers can quickly locate the items that they need.

- **Check-out system:** Implement a check-out and check-in system for equipment. This could be a simple logbook, or a digital system, where teachers record what they have taken and when they plan to return it. This not only ensures accountability, but also helps to keep track of equipment usage.

- **Maintenance:** Regularly inspect and maintain the equipment. Make sure that everything is clean, working properly, and stored in its designated place. If you notice that an item is damaged or missing, make a note of it and take appropriate action.

- **Restock:** Keep track of items that are used frequently and make sure that they are restocked regularly. If an item is running low, order more before it runs out.

- **Update:** Update the inventory, labels and cupboard map as necessary. If new items are added, they should be properly categorised, labelled, and added to the inventory and map.

- **Communicate:** Make sure that all teachers know how the system works. Provide them with a brief training session if necessary. Regularly remind them about the importance of returning items on time and keeping the cupboard tidy.

- **Review and improve:** Regularly review the system and look for ways in which to improve. Ask for feedback from teachers and make adjustments as necessary.

These steps should help to create a well-organised, easy-to-use science resources cupboard that all teachers can benefit from.

Glossary

Acid	A molecule or other entity that can donate a proton or accept an electron pair in reactions. E.g. Lemon juice is sour because it contains citric acid.
Adaptation	The process by which a species becomes better suited to its environment. E.g. The polar bear's white fur is an adaptation that helps it blend in with the snow.
Base	Substances that, in aqueous solution, are slippery to the touch, taste astringent, change the colour of indicators (turns red litmus paper blue), react with acids to form salts, and promote certain chemical reactions. E.g. Soap is a base, which is why it feels slippery.
Biodegradable	Capable of being decomposed by bacteria or other living organisms and thereby avoiding pollution. E.g. Paper is biodegradable, so it breaks down naturally over time without harming the environment.
Biodiversity	The variety of all life forms on earth – the different plants, animals and microorganisms, the genes that they contain and the ecosystems that they form. E.g. The Amazon rainforest has a high level of biodiversity, with thousands of different species of plants and animals.
Carnivore	An animal that feeds on other animals. E.g. Lions are carnivores that hunt and eat other animals.
Chemical change	Any change that results in the formation of new chemical substances. E.g. Burning wood is a chemical change; the wood turns into ash, smoke and gases.
Chemical reaction	A process that leads to the transformation of one set of chemical substances to another. E.g. When baking soda is mixed with vinegar, a chemical reaction occurs, producing bubbles of carbon dioxide gas.
Circulatory system	Also known as the cardiovascular system, this is an organ system that permits blood to circulate and transport nutrients, oxygen, carbon dioxide, hormones and blood cells to and from the cells in the body. E.g. The heart is a key part of the circulatory system, pumping blood throughout the body.
Climate change	A long-term change in the average weather patterns that have come to define Earth's local, regional and global climates. E.g. Rising global temperatures are a key indicator of climate change.
Conclusion	A judgement or decision reached by reasoning based on the information acquired through an investigation or experiment. E.g. After analysing the data from the experiment, the pupils came to the conclusion that plants grow better in sunlight.

Condensation	The change of the physical state of matter from gas phase into liquid phase. E.g. When you see water droplets on the outside of a cold glass, that's condensation.
Conductor	A material that permits a flow of energy. In the case of thermal conductors, they allow heat to flow through and, in electrical conductors, they allow electricity to pass through. E.g. Metal is a good conductor of both heat and electricity.
Conservation	The principle that the total value of a physical quantity (such as energy, mass, or linear momentum) remains constant in a system unless acted upon by external forces. E.g. In a closed system, energy conservation means that the total energy remains constant.
Consumers	Organisms that cannot make their own food and need to consume other organisms. E.g. Rabbits are consumers because they eat plants, but do not produce their own food.
Data	Facts and statistics collected together for reference or analysis. E.g. After the experiment, pupils collected data about the growth of the plants.
Deciduous	Referring to a tree or shrub that sheds its leaves annually. E.g. Oak trees are deciduous; they lose their leaves in the autumn.
Decomposer	Organisms, typically bacteria and fungi, that break down dead or decaying organisms and waste, allowing organic material to be returned to the ecosystem. E.g. Fungi and bacteria are key decomposers in a forest ecosystem, turning dead leaves into nutrients for plants.
Digestive system	A group of organs working together to convert food into energy and basic nutrients to feed the entire body. This includes organs such as the stomach and intestines. E.g. The digestive system processes the food that we eat, extracting nutrients and getting rid of waste.
Dissolve	When something mixes completely into a liquid and seems to disappear. E.g. When you add salt to water and stir, the salt will dissolve and you can't see it anymore.
Eclipse	An astronomical event that occurs when an astronomical object is temporarily obscured. E.g. During a solar eclipse, the Moon passes between the Sun and the Earth, causing the Sun to be fully or partially covered.
Ecosystem	A biological community of interacting organisms and their physical environment. E.g. A forest is an ecosystem with many types of plants and animals interacting with each other.
Electricity	A type of energy resulting from the existence of charged particles such as electrons or protons, either statically as an accumulation of charge, or dynamically as a current. E.g. We use electricity to power our lights, computers and many other devices.

Energy	The capacity to do work, or the property of a system that diminishes when the system does work. E.g. When you eat food, your body gets the energy that it needs to function.
Environment	The surroundings or conditions in which a person, animal, or plant lives or operates. E.g. It's important to take care of our environment and not litter.
Evaporation	The process of a substance in a liquid state changing to a gaseous state due to an increase in temperature or pressure. E.g. When you boil water in a pot, evaporation causes it to turn into steam.
Evergreen	A plant that retains green leaves throughout the year. E.g. Pine trees are evergreen; they stay green even during winter.
Evolution	The process by which different kinds of living organisms are thought to have developed and diversified from earlier forms during the history of the Earth. E.g. Charles Darwin is famous for his theories about evolution.
Experiment	A scientific procedure undertaken to make a discovery, test a hypothesis, or demonstrate a known fact. E.g. The pupils conducted an experiment to determine whether plants grow better in sunlight or darkness.
Fertilisation	The action or process of fertilising an egg, involving the fusion of male and female gametes to form a zygote. E.g. In plants, fertilisation occurs after pollination and leads to the formation of seeds.
Food chain	A series of organisms each dependent on the next as a source of food. E.g. In a simple food chain, grass is eaten by rabbits, and then the rabbits are eaten by foxes.
Food web	A system of interlocking and interdependent food chains. E.g. In a woodland food web, the fox may eat rabbits, squirrels, or birds, and those animals eat a variety of plants.
Force	A push or pull upon an object resulting from the object's interaction with another object. E.g. Gravity is a force that pulls objects toward the Earth.
Fossil fuels	Natural fuels such as coal or gas, formed in the geological past from the remains of living organisms. E.g. Burning fossil fuels such as coal releases carbon dioxide into the atmosphere.
Fossil	The remains or impression of a prehistoric organism preserved in petrified form, or as a mould, or cast in rock. E.g. Scientists found a dinosaur fossil in the desert.
Friction	The resistance that one surface or object encounters when moving over another. E.g. Friction between your shoes and the ground stops you from sliding when you walk.

Gas	A state of matter consisting of particles that have neither a defined volume nor defined shape. E.g. The air that we breathe is a mixture of gases, including oxygen and nitrogen.
Germination	The process by which a plant grows from a seed. E.g. The germination of a seed into a plant begins with the seed absorbing water.
Gravity	The force that attracts a body towards the centre of the Earth, or towards any other physical body having mass. E.g. An apple falling from a tree is due to gravity.
Habitat	The natural home or environment of an animal, plant, or other organism. E.g. The polar bear's habitat is the Arctic.
Herbivore	An animal that eats mostly or only plants, which means that it gets its food from things like leaves, fruits and seeds. Herbivores are important in the food chain because they help to spread seeds and keep plants from growing too much in one area. Examples of herbivores include rabbits, which eat plants like grass, and elephants, which eat plants such as leaves and branches.
Hypothesis	A suggested explanation for an observable phenomenon, or a prediction of a possible causal correlation among multiple phenomena. E.g. Before conducting her science experiment, Sally made a hypothesis about what she thought would happen.
Inheritance	The process by which genetic information is passed on from parent to child. E.g. Inheritance is why pupils often look like their parents.
Insulator	A material that does not easily allow energy to pass through. Thermal insulators reduce the flow of heat and electrical insulators hinder the flow of electricity. E.g. Rubber is an insulator that prevents electricity from passing through.
Invertebrates	Animals that neither possess nor develop a vertebral column, derived from the notochord, commonly known as a backbone or spine. E.g. Snails, spiders and jellyfish are all invertebrates.
Life cycle	The series of changes in the life of an organism, including reproduction. E.g. The life cycle of a butterfly includes stages as an egg, caterpillar, pupa and adult butterfly.
Light	A type of energy that makes it possible for us to see the world around us. E.g. We need light to see. This light can be natural, as from the Sun, or man-made, like from a light bulb.
Liquid	A state of matter with a definite volume but no definite shape. E.g. Water is a liquid at room temperature.
Lunar phase	The shape of the directly sunlit portion of the Moon as viewed from Earth. E.g. The lunar phases change in a regular cycle; the full Moon is one of these phases.

Magnetism	A physical phenomenon resulting in attractive and repulsive forces between objects. E.g. The magnetism of the fridge magnet attracts it to the metal (steel) fridge door.
Mammal	A type of animal that gives birth to live young (not eggs) and feeds them milk. E.g. A dog is a mammal. Cats and humans are also mammals.
Mass	A measure of the amount of matter in an object. E.g. Even though the balloon is big, it has very little mass.
Material	A material is a type of substance or matter from which things can be made. Everything around us is made of different types of materials. For example, a book is made from paper, a window is made from glass, a chair might be made from wood or plastic, and clothes can be made from materials such as cotton or polyester. Materials can have different properties, like being hard or soft, heavy or light, or stretchy or stiff, and these properties help us decide what to use different materials for.
Matter	Anything that has mass and takes up space. It can exist in four states: solid, liquid, gas, or plasma. E.g. Air, water and rocks are all examples of matter.
Metamorphosis	A process by which an animal physically develops after birth or hatching, involving a conspicuous and relatively abrupt change in the animal's body structure. E.g. A butterfly undergoes metamorphosis from a caterpillar into a butterfly.
Microorganisms	A microscopic organism, which may exist in its single-celled form or in a colony of cells. E.g. Bacteria and yeast are types of microorganisms.
Mixture	A combination of two or more substances that are not chemically combined. E.g. Sand and water can be mixed together, but they are still separate substances.
Molecules	The smallest particle in a chemical element or compound that has the chemical properties of that element or compound. Molecules are made up of atoms that are held together by chemical bonds. E.g. A water molecule is made up of two hydrogen atoms and one oxygen atom.
Muscular system	An organ system consisting of skeletal, smooth and cardiac muscles, which allows movement of the body, maintains posture, and circulates blood throughout the body. E.g. When we run, our muscular system is at work.
Nervous system	A network of nerve cells and fibres, which transmits nerve impulses between parts of the body. E.g. The nervous system, which includes the brain and spinal cord, helps us react to our surroundings.

Nutrients	Substances used by organisms to survive, grow and reproduce. E.g. Humans need many different nutrients in their diet, including vitamins, minerals, protein and carbohydrates.
Nutrition	The process of providing or obtaining the food necessary for health and growth. E.g. A balanced diet provides good nutrition.
Omnivore	An animal that eats both plants and other animals, which means that it gets its food from a variety of sources. Omnivores play a special role in the food chain because they can eat different kinds of food, helping to keep both plant and animal populations in balance. Examples of omnivores include bears, which eat berries and fish, and humans, who eat fruits, vegetables and meat.
Orbit	The gravitationally curved trajectory of an object, such as the trajectory of a planet around a star. E.g. It takes one year for the Earth to complete one orbit around the Sun.
pH Scale	A scale used to specify the acidity or basicity of an aqueous solution. E.g. On the pH scale, 7 is neutral, numbers lower than 7 are acidic, and numbers higher than 7 are basic.
Photosynthesis	The process by which green plants and some other organisms use sunlight to synthesise foods with the help of chlorophyll pigments. E.g. Plants use photosynthesis to make food from sunlight, carbon dioxide and water.
Physical change	Changes affecting the form of a chemical substance, but not its chemical composition. E.g. Melting ice into water is a physical change; it's still H_2O before and after.
Plasma	A state of matter similar to gas in which a certain portion of the particles are ionised. It is found in stars and neon lights. E.g. The Sun is made up of plasma.
Pollination	The transfer of pollen from the male part of a flower to the female part, allowing for fertilisation and the production of seeds. E.g. Bees play an important role in pollination.
Population	A group of individuals of the same species living and interbreeding within a given area. E.g. The rabbit population in the field has increased this year.
Predation	The preying of one animal on others. E.g. In the world of birds, predation is common; for instance, hawks often prey on smaller birds or rodents.
Predator	An animal that hunts, catches and eats other animals for food. Predators are important because they help to keep the number of other animals in balance, making sure that there are not too many of one type in an ecosystem. Examples of predators include lions, which eat animals like zebras, and owls, which eat mice and insects.

Prey	An animal that is hunted, caught and eaten by another animal, called a predator. Prey is an important part of the food chain because it provides food for predators, helping to keep the ecosystem healthy and balanced. Examples of prey include zebras, which are eaten by lions, and mice, which are eaten by owls.
Producers	Organisms, primarily plants and algae, that produce food for themselves and other species in an ecosystem, using light energy or chemical energy. E.g. In the ocean, algae are producers that create energy through photosynthesis.
Recycling	The process of converting waste materials into new materials and objects. E.g. By recycling paper, we can save trees.
Renewable energy	Energy that is collected from resources that are naturally replenished on a human timescale, such as sunlight, wind, rain, tides, waves and geothermal heat. E.g. Solar panels generate renewable energy from the Sun.
Reproduction	The process by which new individual organisms – 'offspring' – are produced from their 'parents'. E.g. Reproduction in animals can happen in many ways; some lay eggs, while others give birth to live young.
Respiratory system	A series of organs responsible for taking in oxygen and expelling carbon dioxide. E.g. When we breathe, our respiratory system, including our lungs, helps us to take in oxygen and release carbon dioxide.
Season	A division of the year marked by changes in weather, ecology and the amount of daylight. In many parts of the world, seasons are primarily divided into four types: spring, summer, autumn and winter. E.g. In the season of autumn, leaves on the trees change colour and fall off.
Skeletal system	The framework of the body, consisting of bones and other connective tissues, which protects and supports the body tissues and internal organs. E.g. Our skeleton, part of the skeletal system, provides structure for our bodies.
Solar system	The collection of eight planets and their moons in orbit around the Sun, together with smaller bodies in the form of asteroids, meteoroids and comets. E.g. Earth is part of the solar system, orbiting around the Sun.
Solid	A state of matter characterised by particles arranged such that their shape and volume are relatively stable. E.g. An ice cube is water in a solid state.
Solute	The minor component in a solution, dissolved in the solvent. E.g. When making lemonade, the sugar would be the solute that gets dissolved in the water.

Solution	A homogeneous mixture composed of two or more substances. In such a mixture, a solute is a substance dissolved in another substance, known as a solvent. E.g. When sugar is completely dissolved in water, it forms a solution.
Solvent	A substance that dissolves a solute, resulting in a solution. E.g. Water is a common solvent; it can dissolve many substances.
Sound	A type of energy made by vibrations. When an object vibrates, it causes movement in the particles of the air, which is heard as sound. E.g. The sound of the piano reaches our ears when the piano strings vibrate.
Species	A group of living organisms consisting of similar individuals capable of exchanging genes or interbreeding. E.g. Lions and tigers are different species of big cats.
Temperature	A measure of the warmth or coldness of an object or substance with reference to a standard value. E.g. The temperature of a room can be measured with a thermometer.
Variation	Differences between individuals or groups of organisms of any species caused either by genetic differences or by the effect of environmental factors. E.g. Variation in a species of butterfly might mean that some are blue and some are red.
Vertebrates	Animals that have a backbone or spinal column, including mammals, birds, reptiles, amphibians and fish. E.g. Humans, dogs and birds are all vertebrates because they have backbones.
Water cycle	The cycle of processes by which water circulates between the Earth's oceans, atmosphere and land. It involves precipitation, evaporation, condensation and transpiration. E.g. Rain is part of the water cycle. It falls from the sky, is absorbed into the ground, and eventually evaporates back into the sky.

BV - #0190 - 171125 - C151 - 297/210/7 - PB - 9781915615305 - Gloss Lamination